YES YOU CAN!

Make Stunning Quilts From Simple Patterns

Judy Martin

CROSLEY-GRIFFITH
PUBLISHING COMPANY, INC.
1321 Broad Street
Grinnell, Iowa 50112
(515) 236-4854

To Steve, Kate, and Will

ACKNOWLEDGMENTS: Special thanks to Don and Mollie Bennett. Thanks also to Steve for his patience during this project and for the many little things he does. Thanks to Marsha McCloskey and Louise O. Townsend for their friendship over the years and for feedback when I needed it. Finally, thanks to the wonderful quilters who keep quilting alive and who are a constant source of inspiration to me.

Written and illustrated by Judy Martin
Quilts designed and made by Judy Martin
Photography by Brian Birlauf, Birlauf Steen Photography

ISBN 0-929589-02-5
Published by Crosley-Griffith Publishing Company, Inc.
1321 Broad Street, Grinnell, Iowa 50112
First Printing 1992
15 14 13 12 11 10 9 8 7 6 5 4 3 2

CONTENTS

Introduction

I have made hundreds of quilts over the course of 23 years, and although I am capable of making quilts in the trickiest patterns, nothing pleases me more than making a stunning quilt from a simple pattern. There is something very relaxing and rejuvenating about a project that goes along without a snag. It is the way leisure time should be spent. Every quilter deserves to experience the very special pleasure of making easy quilts that are beautiful, worthwhile, and satisfying. And that is why I wrote this book.

The quilts in this book don't look like the easy quilts you have seen before. They have charm, individuality, and intricacy--qualities often found in antique quilts but usually lacking in quickie projects. I know you aren't going to believe how quickly and easily you can make these gorgeous quilts, so let me take a moment to anticipate your questions and explain how this book will enable you to make stunning quilts from simple patterns.

"I never thought I had the time or experience to make such fabulous quilts. Can I really make these?"

YES YOU CAN! Quilts that *look* too beautiful to be easy are the point of this book. Rather than making the quilts easy by virtue of large patches or overly simple shapes, I have designed the quilts in this book to be easy in more subtle ways. The size and number of patches is just one part of what makes a quilt easy. Taking advantage of clever shortcuts and designing for easy joints are two of the more important factors. All of the quilts in this book are easy to cut and sew using the latest shortcuts. The number of patches is modest, although not as minimal as you may find in some publications. I wanted to include quilts that had a special quality not possible in a "Make-a-Quilt-This-Instant" project. After all, isn't it really more satisfying to spend an extra day or two to make a truly wonderful quilt? Your quilt will be more impressive, and you alone--not everyone who sees your quilt--will know just how easy it was to make.

"How will I know what is easy?"

Without the telltale giant patches, you may need some help to see what makes these quilts easy. For this reason, I have included a brief section called "What Makes This Quilt Easy" at the beginning of each pattern. The quilts in this book were designed with simplicity in mind. You can count on being able to master any one of them.

"I love the old-time charm of Scrap Quilts and the speed of modern rotary cutting. Can I have it both ways?"

YES YOU CAN! I, too, love Scrap Quilts, and I wasn't willing to endorse any shortcut that compromised the true Scrap Quilt look I was after. Now that I have perfected the Short Strips technique, I can honestly say that old-fashioned methods are no longer the only way to make a *real* Scrap Quilt.

"I see you are introducing a new technique for rotary cutting. Do I need a whole new set of tools for this?"

Not at all. Short Strips improves upon old rotary cutting methods, but it does not require any new tools. All you need are a mat, a cutter, and an ordinary rotary ruler. If you are experienced with speedy techniques, you won't need a whole new mindset, just a few new details that make a world of difference. If rotary cutting didn't suit you in the past, take another look. The Short Strips technique answers the problems of grain and pattern alignment, and it is easy to learn and easy to use without rethinking your whole approach to quiltmaking.

"I prefer traditional methods. Can I still make quilts from these patterns?"

YES YOU CAN! Every quilt in this book is presented with accurate, full-size patterns and complete directions for rotary cutting as well as traditional methods. On all pattern patches you will find seam allowances, grain arrows, and points trimmed for easy piecing. Yardage and cutting charts are presented two ways for easy reference no matter what method you choose.

"These directions look long! Do I need a degree in Quiltmaking to follow them?"

Of course not! The length of the directions is due to their completeness, not their difficulty. Most of these patterns are presented in three different sizes. Every detail, from what patches you sew first to which way you press the seam allowances, is covered in the step-by-step narrative. If you are an experienced quilter, you can skip these instructions altogether and use the handy "At-A-Glance" charts and diagrams to see exactly how to make each quilt. Even if you have been quilting for years, though, it is comforting to know the help is there if you need it.

"I'm a little unsure about choosing colors and fabrics. Can I come up with a color scheme that really works for my quilt?"

YES YOU CAN! A full-page color photograph of each quilt shows every detail. You can easily see just how I combined colors and fabrics for the quilts. The "Scrap Sense & Color Confidence" chapter provides further guidance. I describe my color choices and suggest additional color schemes for each quilt, as well. Fabrics corresponding to these additional color schemes are photographed on pages 47-48. It is really very simple to choose a successful color scheme when everything is laid out so clearly.

"Do I need a big collection of scraps to make these quilts?"

Not really. If you like the scrap look but don't have much fabric on hand, you can buy fat quarters and short lengths of fabric to make your first scrap quilt and have some left over to start building your stash for future projects. If you prefer to make quilts from just a few fabrics, you will find yardage listings to guide you. It is a simple matter of using just one fabric in each listed color rather than using a whole range of scraps.

"In this one book can I find all the information and inspiration I need to make stunning quilts from simple patterns?"

YES YOU CAN!

SHORT STRIPS & ROTARY PATCHES, SHORTCUTS TO STUNNING QUILTS

After years of scissor cutting, I became a rotary-cutting convert. I resisted rotary cutting for a long time because I was uncomfortable with some of the limitations of the usual strip-cutting and strip-piecing methods. What bothered me most about rotary cutting was the reliance on crosswise grain. With strip piecing, I disliked the lack of flexibility in using scrap fabrics. I devised my own quick rotary methods to solve these problems. I call my techniques Short Strips and Rotary Patches. Now I enjoy the speed and accuracy of rotary cutting, and I avoid the painful calluses that I used to develop when I was cutting for days on end with scissors.

THE BASIC SHORT STRIPS METHOD

You will need a rotary cutter, a cutting mat, and a rotary ruler. A rotary cutter is a rolling wheel blade attached to a handle. It looks like a pizza cutter or a tracing wheel, but it is much sharper. (Take care: these blades are razor-sharp! Always keep your rotary cutter out of reach of children and shield the blade when not in use. Keep your fingers well back from the path of the cutter to avoid injury.) A cutting mat will protect your cutting surface and preserve your blade. You will run the rotary cutter along the edge of the rotary ruler. Your ruler should be transparent, 24" long, be ruled at ⅛" intervals, and have a crisp, straight edge that will guide the blade without being damaged by it. Additional, smaller rulers come in handy. For short crosswise cuts, a small ruler is long enough and it is easier to manipulate. However, only the one large ruler is required.

The method is easy. You simply layer four or five pieces of fabric, each 18" long, aligning selvedges. Use your rotary ruler and cutter to trim off the selvedge and cut 18" Short Strips of the widths needed to make your patches. Rotary rulers are generally 24" long to accommodate 45"-wide fabric folded in half. You can use the same ruler to cut 18" Short Strips in a single stroke without having to shift the ruler. Strip width measurements are the same as for typical rotary cutting.

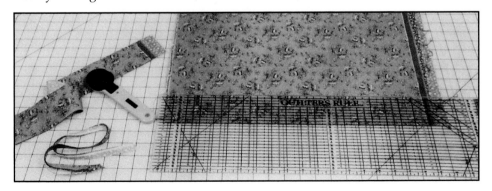

Layer four fabrics, with the selvedges or lengthwise grain at the front of the table. Trim the selvedges. (Be careful! Some are deeper than others!) Use your rotary ruler to measure and cut Short Strips the full 18" length by whatever width you desire.

ADVANTAGES OF SHORT STRIPS

Rather than cutting 45"-long strips across the width of the folded fabric, you cut Short Strips parallel to the selvedges. Single layers of fabric stack better than folded fabrics, for more perfect cuts. So with Short Strips you can layer four different single layers of fabric for perfect cutting, whereas conventional rotary cutting would have you layer two folded fabrics to achieve the same total of four layers, but with a bit of a hump at the two folds.

Their shorter length makes Short Strips easier to manage, and you avoid the crease (and the occasional kink in your supposedly straight edge) when you don't have the fold to contend with.

The Short Strips technique allows you to take advantage of the more stable lengthwise grain for the long edges of your patches. Furthermore, the print always aligns better with the lengthwise grain, so Short Strips ensure the best possible appearance for each patch. When making Scrap Quilts from Short Strips, you can layer four different fabrics, with solids and all-over prints on the bottom layers and stripes, plaids, or other fabrics that need careful alignment on the top. You can follow the stripe or other pattern when you position your rotary ruler. (With conventional rotary cutting, the fabric is doubled, so you must cut half of each fabric--even difficult prints or stripes--from an unseen lower layer, risking poor alignment.

When layering fabrics for Short Strips, place the fabrics that require careful alignment on the top of the stack. That way, you can position your rotary ruler along the stripe, plaid, or linear printed pattern for cutting.

Conventional rotary cutting and Short Strips provide approximately the same time savings over traditional methods. With Short Strips, you will need about twice as many strips, but you can cut each twice as fast, since conventional rotary cutting yields two strips from each four layers, whereas Short Strips yields four strips from four layers. One advantage of Short Strips is that, since the strips are shorter, you will need more of them. That means you can use more different fabrics for each kind of strip, so your Scrap Quilts will look scrappier.

For Short Strips, the width of the fabric doesn't matter. You can mix 36" widths with 42" or 45" widths, or you can use whatever width remains after having used some of the fabric for another project.

Fabrics layered for Short Strips can vary in width. Feel free to mix remnants with 36" and 45" wide pieces.

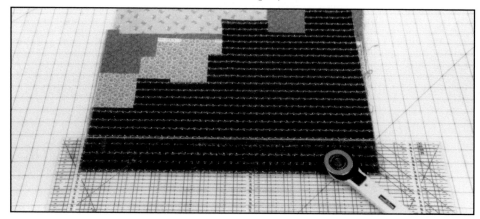

If you have been hesitant to try rotary cutting because of the grain considerations or other differences from your usual quiltmaking methods, try Short Strips. You'll be thrilled at the ease and accuracy of this method and surprised to find it is not as intimidating as you might have thought.

MINI STRIPS

For a very scrappy look, you may not need more than one strip of each fabric in the quilt. When your quilt doesn't have many patches of a particular size, shape, and color, such as when it is a very small quilt or when there is only one such patch per block, Short Strips may not provide enough variety for a Scrap Quilt. In such cases, you can cut Mini Strips, just 9" long, in order to double the variety of fabrics used for such patches. You can also use Mini Strips when you have on hand quarter-yard pieces that you want to use in your quilt. If you can't buy a ready-cut fat quarter, sometimes you may want to buy a quarter-yard length of fabric, rather than a half yard off the bolt. Simply layer these shorter pieces with each other, and cut lengthwise Mini Strips. The patches that you cut from Mini Strips are indistinguishable from those that you cut from Short Strips.

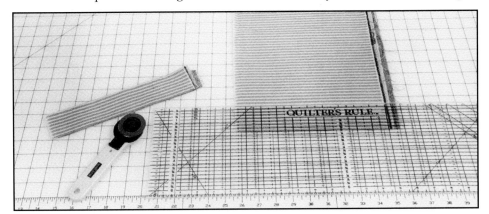

When you wish to use ¼-yard pieces rather than ½-yard ones, stack them together and cut 9" Mini Strips rather than Short Strips. You will need about twice as many of these Mini Strips.

THE BASIC ROTARY PATCH METHOD

Rather than using my Short Strips for strip piecing, I prefer to use them another way. I call the method Rotary Patches. You simply cut stacks of Short Strips; then, before you start sewing, you cut the stacks of Short Strips further into the squares, rectangles, triangles, or other patches needed for the quilt.

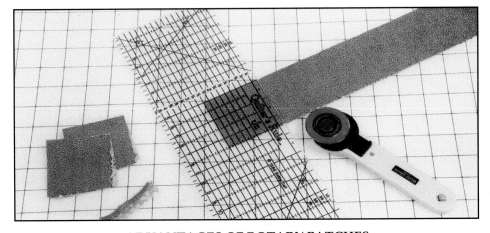

Use your rotary ruler to cut Short Strips crosswise into patches in the dimensions needed.

ADVANTAGES OF ROTARY PATCHES

Strip piecing does not save any cutting. It simply postpones some of it. Here is my reasoning: You are going to have to do exactly the same amount of cutting regardless of whether you make the final cuts before or after sewing strips. That is, if your quilt comprises 400 squares, you will have cut around all four sides of each of the 400 squares before you are finished--one way or the other. Strip piecing does save on the number of pieces of fabric that you must feed into the sewing machine. But there are also some drawbacks to strip piecing. You can't reinforce each seam with backstitching. (I find this a problem especially now that I have two toddlers who love to get their hands on my quilts in progress. Their loving attention can unravel a seam in no time if it isn't reinforced with a backstitch.)

Another drawback to strip piecing is that you must cut across seam allowances when you cut the pieced strips into units later. You may find it difficult to be perfectly accurate when you are cutting across seams. Furthermermore, usually you can cut through just one layer at a time when you cut across seams.

By cutting Rotary Patches from your strips before sewing, you can do all of the cutting easily and precisely through four to six layers. You will make up the time lost in sewing a greater number of pieces by cutting through many layers at once. With Rotary Patches, all of the strips can be different lengths. (For strip piecing, you will need similar lengths for the strips to be joined together.) The Rotary Patches technique, unlike strip piecing, allows you to use true scraps and fabric remnants. Furthermore, you can mix up the scraps more thoroughly, you can backstitch the ends of every seam, and you can piece in the traditional sequence without thinking ahead as you would have to for strip piecing.

If you have been strip piecing, try Rotary Patches. It is a real pleasure to spend just a little time and be all done--not just half done--with the cutting.

BUYING FABRIC FOR SHORT STRIPS SCRAP QUILTS

You can buy all-new fabric to make the Short Strips projects in this book. Buy ½-yard pieces or fat quarters when 18"-long Short Strips are indicated. (Fat quarters are 18" long by half the fabric width. One of these is the equivalent of ¼ yard, but the piece is more square, being twice as long on the lengthwise grain and half as wide as the usual ¼-yard piece.) Buy ¼-yard pieces when 9" Mini Strips are required. If you buy all-new fabric, you will have quite a bit left over for future projects. In order to get the desired scrap look, you will want to cut just a few Short Strips from each fabric. (And it is delightful to have clean, straight edges on your leftovers!)

USING FABRIC ON HAND FOR SHORT STRIPS & ROTARY PATCHES

You can also use scraps, leftovers, and other fabric on hand. Odd pieces may need a little preparation before you use them for Short Strips.

You may have several yards each of some fabrics. You will find them easier to handle if you cut off a half yard or a fat quarter to layer with your other fabrics for cutting Short Strips.

Cut off an 18" length or a fat quarter to use for Short Strips. This makes large pieces easy to manage.

If you need the full length of your fabric for borders, cut the borders first, then cut a half-yard length of the remaining width for Short Strips.

If you want to conserve fabric length for some as-yet undetermined project, cut off one or more 18" lengths just the width of a single strip.

To conserve the full fabric length, cut off one or more narrow pieces 18" long and just one strip wide.

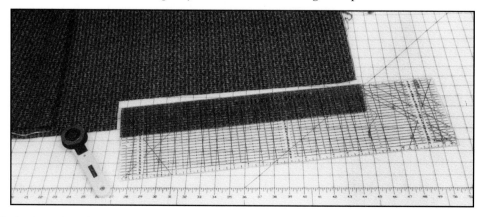

If your fabric on hand has been used for projects before, it may have ragged edges--perhaps a square or triangular hole cut out of the corner. You will need to make a clean edge so you can layer this fabric with the others and cut strips. You can make a clean cut at the original center fold of the fabric. This gives you two clean-cut pieces to work with. You don't have any useless, ragged scrap to toss or save. Since the center crease often resists any attempt to iron it out, you may do best to avoid it altogether. In view of this, cutting at the fold doesn't waste any fabric at all.

Make a clean-cut edge on ragged leftovers by cutting the piece in two along the original center crease.

Sometimes, your fabric on hand will be very long and narrow. Perhaps you have cut out wide borders, leaving a piece three yards long and just a few inches wide. Cut the remnant into several 18" lengths to correspond to the number of strips you need. Layer as many as four of these lengths of a single fabric, aligning the clean-cut edges. When you cut Rotary Patches from this stack, you will get the same results as if you had layered the fabric with others to cut several strips off the width.

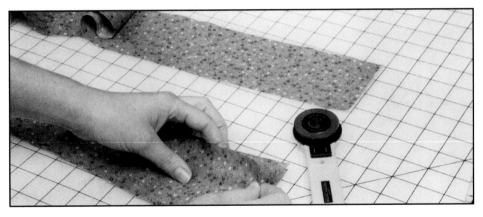

Long, narrow remnants should be cut into 18" lengths. Stack these together to enable you to cut as many strips as you cut from wider pieces.

TIMESAVING TIPS & HELPFUL HINTS

Whenever possible, cut a variety of different Rotary Patch shapes from a single Short Strip. For example, you might cut a 1½" x 18" strip to make one 1½" x 4½" rectangle, one 1½" x 6½" rectangle, and four 1½" squares. This makes the most efficient use of uniform strips, and it allows you to mix the fabrics more thoroughly throughout a Scrap Quilt.

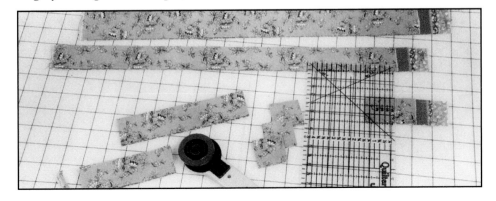

For the best scrap effect, especially in Log Cabin Quilts, cut a variety of different-sized patches requiring the same strip width from a single strip.

Occasionally, you may want to cut lengthwise strips that are a little longer than 18". For example, Red Sky at Night calls for E patches that are 18½" long by 2½" wide. Ordinary Short Strips won't do. You will need to cut strips 18½" long for these. Of course, border strips will be longer than 18", as well. I don't like to seam borders unnecessarily, so my directions allow enough yardage for seamless borders. You will want to cut borders first. That way, you will be sure to have a piece long enough for seamless borders.

In general, try to keep the strips shorter than 24" so you won't have to shift the ruler when you cut. You may want to adjust the strip length to accommodate particular patches. For example if you need to cut 1½" x 12½" rectangles, there is no need to make the strips 18" long. Make them 12½" instead. For 1½" x 6½" rectangles, cut strips 19½" or 20" long so you can fit three rectangles end to end.

Strips need not be 18" or even 9" in length. Depending on what fabric is at hand and what patches are called for, you may want longer or shorter strips. Sort fabrics into stacks of similar length for the most efficient cutting.

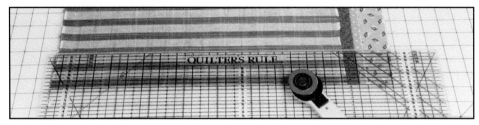

You can cut a strip 4" long or 12" long or whatever your scrap of fabric will allow. In fact, you can layer four different-sized pieces of fabric, and cut them all at once. You simply need to make a clean cut on one lengthwise edge of each fabric and align the clean-cut edges of four fabrics when you layer them.

You may find it helpful to sort fabrics beyond just their color categories, grouping ones of a similar length for cutting together. That way, you will always be cutting through all four layers. You won't waste strokes by cutting through fewer layers when longer fabrics extend beyond shorter ones in the same stack. (Don't get carried away with this to the point of grouping different-colored fabrics just because they are the same length. You still need to keep them sorted according to which patches need to be cut from them.)

The rotary cutting chart for each pattern in this book lists cutting plans for use with 18" strips in most cases. Occasionally, 9" strips are called for. If you are using odd-sized scraps, you can still follow the rotary cutting chart for strip widths and cross cuts. However, you may have fewer cross cuts from a stack of fabrics, and the patch yield per strip will differ. You will just need to make up the remaining cross cuts and patches from other strips. Keeping track will be a little more involved if you stray from the plan in the book. You can make a checklist with headings for each shape, size, and color of patch, and tally the patches as you cut them. (Remember to count all four layers!) You can refer to the yardage chart (above the rotary cutting chart) for the needed patch totals.

STEP-BY-STEP DIRECTIONS FOR SHORT STRIPS & ROTARY PATCHES

If you are accustomed to rotary cutting, it is easy to make the changeover to Short Strips and Rotary Patches. Just as for rotary cutting, you lay out the fabric on your cutting table with the selvedges or clean-cut lengthwise edges along the front edge of the table. Instead of making strokes away from your body, though, you will place the ruler parallel to the front edge of the table and cut from side to side (from right to left if you are right-handed or from left to right if you are left-handed). The resulting strips have the lengthwise grain on the long edge. The strip measurements and patch dimensions don't change. Only the grain changes.

Start by cutting Short Strips: Layer four fabrics, aligning selvedges or clean-cut edges along the front of the cutting surface or angling them slightly. Use your rotary ruler to measure and cut from side to side to make lengthwise strips.

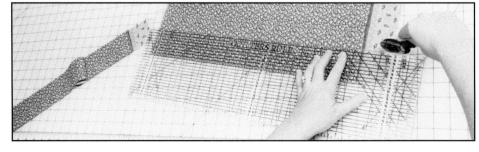

For squares, you still cut strips the finished measurement plus ½" for seam allowances. You then cut strips at intervals equal to the strip width to complete the squares.

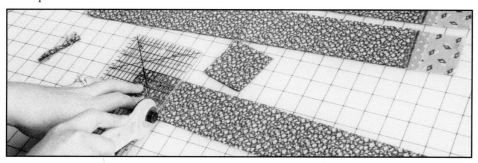

For squares, cut Short Strips the width of the patch, allowing for seams. Make cross cuts at intervals of this same measurement to complete squares.

For isosceles right triangles having the straight grain on the short side, cut strips the finished size of a short side plus ⅞". Cut the strips into squares, cutting at intervals equal to the strip width. Then cut these squares into triangles by placing a rotary ruler diagonally from corner to corner of a stack of squares. Cut along the ruler to form two stacks of triangles.

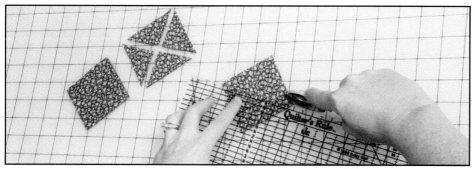

For isosceles right triangles, cut Short Strips of a width equal to the finished dimension of the short side of the triangle plus ⅞". Then make cross cuts at the same interval to make squares. Cut these in half diagonally to make triangles.

For isosceles right triangles having the straight grain on the long edge, cut strips 18" long by the finished dimension of the long side plus 1¼". Use this same measurement to cut at intervals to form squares. Cut each stack of squares in half diagonally, placing the ruler from corner to corner. Leave the patches in place and position the ruler on the opposite diagonal, from corner to corner, and cut again. You now have four stacks of triangles.

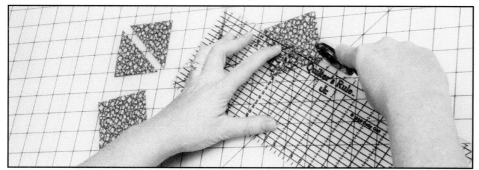

For isosceles right triangles having the straight grain on the long side, cut Short Strips of a width equal to the finished dimension of the long side of the triangle plus 1¼". Then make cross cuts at the same interval to make squares. Cut squares in half along both diagonals to make triangles.

Rectangles are cut from strips ½" wider than the finished dimension of a short side. Strips are cut at intervals equal to the long side plus ½" to make rectangles.

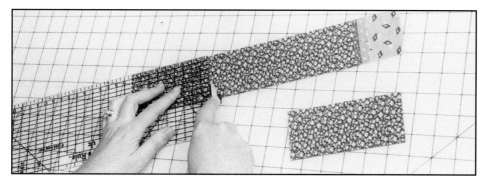

For rectangles, cut Short Strips the width of the rectangle, allowing for seams. Make cross cuts at intervals equal to the patch length, allowing for seams, to complete rectangles.

Trapezoids, octagons, rhombuses, and other unusual shapes can be cut using a combination of ordinary strips and paper patterns taped to your rotary ruler. Simple shapes with dimensions not found on standard rulers can also be cut this way. The principle is easy. Where angles and dimensions are easily reproduced with ruler markings, use them. When they are not, tape a pattern to your ruler and use it as a guide for aligning the cut edge of your fabric. How you place the pattern on your ruler depends on which part needs cutting. In any case, tape the pattern, face down, to the underside of the ruler. This way, it will be face up when you turn the ruler over, and the pattern will rest right against the fabric to guide you in cutting perfectly. Sometimes two perpendicular edges need cutting. You can tape the patch with one edge along the top of the ruler and one edge along the side to cut two edges without repositioning the ruler.

For trapezoids, such as the C patch for Wind in My Sails (pages 88-92), cut Short Strips the width of the patch, allowing for seam allowances. In this case, cut strips 18" long and 2⅜" wide. Tape the pattern to the ruler with the two short ends at the top and side of the ruler. (For large trapezoids, you may need a 12" square rotary ruler to do this. Alternatively, you can tape the pattern to your usual ruler with one short end even with the top of the ruler and the opposite end of the pattern extending beyond the ruler. You will need to reposition the ruler for the second cut in this case.) Align the long edges of the pattern with the long edges of a stack of four Short Strips. One short end of the pattern should be at one end of the strip. Cut the two ends of the patch even with the edges of the ruler. Rotate the remainder of the stack of strips and align three sides of the pattern with the fabric. Make a single cut to complete the second stack of trapezoid patches. Continue cutting in this manner until the strip runs out.

For trapezoids, cut Short Strips the width of the patch, allowing for seams. Then tape the pattern to your ruler as shown, and cut the two short ends along the ruler.

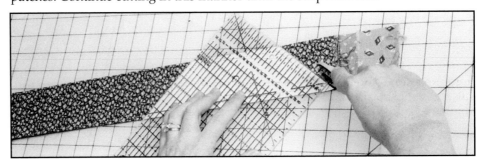

For octagons, such as the F patch for Wedding Memories (pages 93-96), cut strips the width of the patch, allowing for seam allowances. The length of the strips for large patches like this one should be some multiple of the patch width. In this case, cut strips 19" long and 9½" wide. Cut the strip crosswise at 9½" to make two squares. Tape the octagon pattern to the ruler with two of the longer sides along the top and side of the ruler. A half octagon pattern, as presented on page 96 will suffice; you don't need to draw the other half. (For large octagons, you may want to use a 12" square rotary ruler. If you don't have a large square ruler, you can tape the pattern to your usual ruler with one edge even with the top of the ruler and the other edge of the pattern extending beyond the ruler. You will need to reposition the ruler for the second cut in this case.) Align the short edges of the pattern with the edges of a stack of four 9½" squares. Cut two ends of the patch even with the edges of the ruler. Rotate the stack of squares and align the pattern with the other half of the same squares. Make two more cuts to complete the stack of octagon patches. Cut all of the squares in this way.

For octagons, cut Short Strips the width of the patch, allowing for seams. Then cut each strip crosswise into squares. Tape the pattern (a half octagon will suffice) to your ruler as shown, and cut off two corners along the ruler. Rotate the fabric, realign the ruler, and cut off the remaining two corners.

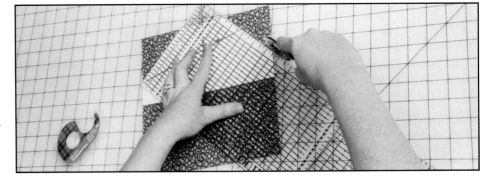

For rhombuses having the straight grain on the parallel sides, such as the F and I patches for Katherine's Bouquet (pages 57-61) and the A and B patches for Summerfest (pages 79-82), cut Short Strips the width of the patch, allowing for seam allowances. In the case of the I patch for Katherine's Bouquet, cut strips 18" long and 2⅜" wide. Cut the strips crosswise to form rectangles big enough for two rhombuses, in this case, 7¾". (This measurement is a little generous, since the actual dimension won't be found on any ruler. The extra length won't matter because you will be cutting an accurate rhombus from each end, leaving a sliver in the middle.) Tape the pattern to the ruler with the diagonal end along the top of the ruler. Align the remaining three edges of the pattern with one end of a stack of four rectangles. Cut the diagonal end of the patch even with the edge of the ruler. Rotate the fabric stack and align three sides of the pattern with the remaining end of the rectangles. Trim the end along the ruler to complete the second stack of rhombus patches. Continue cutting rhombuses in this manner from all of the rectangles.

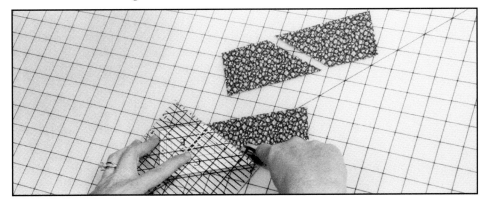

For rhombuses having the straight grain along the parallel sides, cut Short Strips the width of the patch, allowing for seams. Cut the strips crosswise into rectangles big enough for two rhombuses. Tape the pattern to your ruler as shown, and cut along the ruler. Align the ruler over the other half to shave off the end.

For rhombuses having the straight grain on the diagonal end, such as the C patch for Road to Colorado (pages 66-70) and the B patch in Cobblestones (pages 101-104), cut Short Strips wide enough for two patches end to end, allowing for seam allowances. Round up to a slightly larger number if necessary to have a measurement that you will find on your ruler. (The extra will be shaved off for a perfectly accurate patch when you make the final cut.) In the case of the C patch for Road to Colorado, cut strips 18" long and 5¼" wide. Cut at a 45° angle to remove a 5¼" triangle from the lower right corner of the stack of strips. Align your rotary ruler with this diagonally cut end and cut at intervals of 2½". (This is the width of the rhombus, allowing for seam allowances.) In this case, you can cut three of these parallelograms from each strip. Tape the rhombus pattern to the ruler with the short, square end along the top of the ruler. Align the remaining three edges of the pattern with one end of a stack of four parallelograms. Cut the patch even with the edge of the ruler. Rotate the fabric stack and align three sides of the pattern with the remaining end of the parallelogram. Trim the end along the ruler to complete the second stack of rhombus patches. Continue cutting rhombuses in this manner from all of the parallelograms.

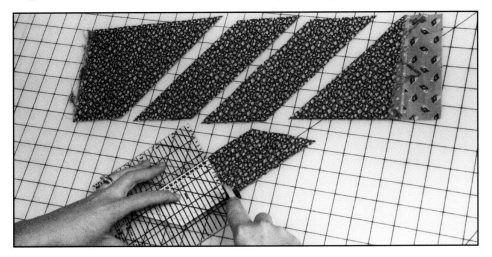

For rhombuses having the straight grain along the angled end, cut Short Strips wide enough for two patches end to end. Cut off one corner at 45°. Then cut at intervals equal to the patch width, allowing for seams. This makes parallelograms. Tape the pattern to your ruler as shown. Align the fabric stack of parallelograms with the pattern, and cut along the ruler. Turn the fabric, realign the ruler, and trim the end of the remainder of the parallelogram.

TRIMMING THE POINTS OF ROTARY PATCHES FOR EASY PIECING

Since there are no marked seam lines on Rotary Patches, you may want to trim the points of the patches to help you align them perfectly for machine piecing. The full-size patterns for each quilt show where to trim the points. The idea is to cut off points so that neighboring patches can be aligned perfectly for seaming simply by matching their ends. You can trim points by tracing a full-size pattern with the points trimmed as indicated. Tape the pattern to the underside of your rotary ruler with the trimmed point at the top edge of the ruler. Align the ruler over your stack of four Rotary Patches and cut along the ruler to trim the points. After trimming this point off all patches, reposition the pattern on the ruler for the remaining points.

To trim the points for odd-shaped patches, such as the pointy B triangle of Wedding Memories (pages 93-96), tape the pattern to your rotary ruler with the trim line at the top of the ruler. Align the pattern with your stack of Rotary Patches, and cut along the ruler's edge.

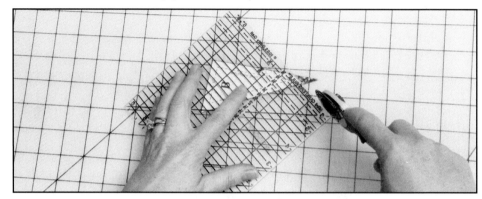

For some shapes, you can tape the pattern with one trimmed point at the top of the ruler and another at the side to cut off both points without repositioning the ruler or pattern.

Once you grow accustomed to the point-trimming process, you can trim the points of many shapes without tracing a pattern. Instead, you can simply align the stack of Rotary Patches with ruler markings and cut along the edge of the ruler. With practice, you will learn just what measurements are right for each size and shape of patch. For many shapes, you will be cutting the point off at the measurement corresponding to the finished side plus ½". This is the case for isosceles right triangles having the short side on the straight grain. It is also true for rhombuses such as the A patch for Summerfest (page 82), photographed below. For these, you simply align the appropriate rulings with the edges of the patch and cut along the top of the ruler.

For many patches, such as the A patch for Summerfest shown, you can trim points without tracing a pattern. Simply align the stack of Rotary Patches with the appropriate ruler markings, and trim the point along the top of the ruler. In this example, the rhombus has a finished length of 4". The short end of the stack of Rotary Patches is aligned with the 4½" ruling to trim the point along the ruler's edge.

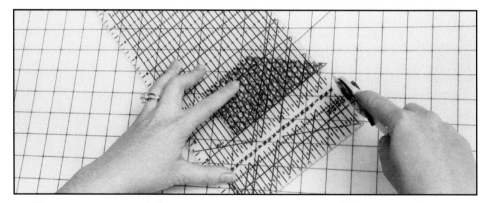

If you are unsure of the measurement, you can simply lay your clear rotary ruler over the full-size pattern in the book, with one or more trimmed points at the edge(s) of the ruler. Notice the rulings that align with the edges of the pattern. Place the ruler in exactly the same position over your Rotary Patches to trim their points. (If the patch edges do not fall on rule lines, you can trace the pattern and tape it to the ruler, as described above.) To make your sewing easy, there is nothing like a perfectly cut Rotary Patch with points trimmed for natural alignment. The time you take trimming points now will be time saved in sewing later.

SCRAP SENSE &
COLOR CONFIDENCE

CAN'T-MISS COLOR SCHEMES

Your choice of colors can affect your quilt profoundly, but the prospect need not intimidate you. If choosing colors for a quilt has been a problem for you in the past, don't worry. In this book, you will find a large color photograph of each quilt to guide you in color selection. If you prefer different colors from those I used to make a quilt, you will find additional appropriate color schemes listed for each of the patterns. Fabrics grouped in many of these color schemes are photographed on pages 47-48. (You will want to use more fabrics than I had room to show on these two pages, but you can easily add fabrics to fit within the range of colors photographed.) Surely you will find something that pleases you with all of these ideas to choose from. After all, the object is not to choose the "right" colors; it is not to choose the most popular colors; the object is to choose a color scheme that *you* like. How hard can it be to recognize a color scheme that you like when you see it?

For many of you, choosing colors and fabrics is the most enjoyable step in making a quilt. It is here that you get to exercise your creativity, to add your own personal touches to a pattern. If color is your forté, I invite you to "do your own thing" with the patterns in this book. Have fun!

SCRAP SENSE & FABULOUS FABRIC CHOICES

Everyone loves a Scrap Quilt. Each print seems to have a story of its own, and the mix of prints tells so much about the time in which the quilt was made. Scrap Quilts made today will be treasured years hence for their glimpse into the past. Scrap fabrics add nuances of color, shading, and visual texture that give depth and richness to a quilt.

For quilters like me, who revel in quilt planning and color selection, the routine of actually making the quilt can get a little boring. Scrap Quilts offer the opportunity of extending our enjoyment all through the process. With a Scrap Quilt, you are never done with the planning until the last patch is in place!

This planning is not difficult. It is simply a matter of making a series of tiny judgments. To make a Scrap Quilt, you will start by choosing a pattern. Next you will need to plan which colors to include and how far each color should range. Then you will select fabrics and sort them by color or value. You will decide where to place the colors in the quilt plan, and finally, where to put individual fabrics.

Many of these judgments are spur-of-the-moment decisions made as you sew. You will be constantly considering which fabrics to put next to each other. After the blocks are completed, you will need to plan the best sequence of blocks across the quilt surface, taking into account the color balance.

Some quilters "audition" each patch on a design wall. Most don't agonize over every little decision, though. Usually, a quick and easy judgment will do. Even if you plan to be completely random about it, I think you will find yourself sometimes vetoing patch combinations and looking for something more suitable. After all, this is *your* quilt, and you want it to be just so. Every decision makes your quilt a little more of a personal statement. Every choice you make affects the whole. Every detail that you consider (and some that you don't even think about) becomes a thread in the intricate weave of the quilt surface.

Every small detail that you think through is there in your quilt to give pleasure to anyone who cares to look closely. The new shapes that suggest themselves where adjacent patches blend a little more than usual; the lovely pairing of two unlikely prints in neighboring patches; the unique way you interpret colors and make use of prints--all of these layer your quilt with a delightful complexity just inviting exploration and awaiting discovery.

Once you have selected a color scheme, you can begin choosing a palette of fabrics. Choose a range of fabrics in each color needed for the quilt. That is, choose fabrics that dance around the average color impression of your plan. If your plan calls for red, you may want to include cinnamon brown and turkey red balanced by coral and dark rose. If you prefer a lighter touch, temper bright, clear reds with softer tones like salmon and bubble gum pink. Feel free to include fabrics with a variety of sizes and types of prints: basic dots, stripes, plaids, and other rhythmic geometrics; widely spaced motifs; viney, packed prints; voluptuous florals; soft, watercolor effects; large prints; and tiny calicoes. Don't worry about including every type of print if you have strong preferences or aversions. Your personality will come through in your choices and give your quilt individuality. Stretch a little with your colors. Don't match them too carefully or your quilt won't look like a Scrap Quilt. Every fabric need not be a current favorite. The overall mix is more important than any single fabric.

When you have gathered the fabrics, spread them out in a staggered array to see how they look together. Eliminate any that don't seem to work. Then decide if you have enough fabrics to develop your quilt according to plan. The number of different fabrics in a Scrap Quilt can vary tremendously. The Scrap Quilts in this book generally have 100-150 fabrics. For smaller quilts, you can get away with fewer fabrics. For larger quilts you may need more. The actual number of fabrics has less to do with how scrappy a quilt looks than you might think. Summerfest looks especially scrappy with its random, multicolored fabrics. In fact, it has fewer different fabrics than Heart & Home in its three colors. How scrappy a quilt looks depends on the number of different colors, how uniformly the colors are placed, and how far each color ranges, not just on how many fabrics are included.

When I am making a Scrap Quilt, I don't plan on a certain number of fabrics. The number depends on what I have available. First I plan which colors I intend to use, and I get out all of the appropriate fabrics from my stash. Then, whether or not I have plenty of suitable fabrics, I make a trip to my local quilt shop for additional fabrics in these colors. This improves the mix in the quilt and, even more importantly, it replenishes fabrics before I use them. The more different fabrics I have, the less of each I must use. When I don't need to use the last little bit of any fabric, the variety in my stash grows, rather than diminishes.

Often, I will adjust my fabric selection according to the cutting requirements. For example, if I am making Heart & Home (page 51) in the large size, and I have 50 rose prints, I would eliminate ten of them, so I can cut a single strip from each of 40 fabrics. If I had 19 rose fabrics, I would buy one more and cut two strips from each fabric. The yardage and cutting chart for each quilt lists a suggested number of fabrics to use for each size. These numbers take into account the number of strips that you will be cutting. You can use any number of fabrics that you desire. If you are cutting Short Strips, however, it will be easier to do if you use no more fabrics than the total number of strips in any given color.

Obviously, it is helpful to have a stash of fabrics on hand if you plan to make Scrap Quilts. If you try to construct a Scrap Quilt from fabrics that you can find at the store at any given moment, you may end up with a less-than-perfect mix. Too many fabrics will be from coordinated lines that match too well to look scrappy; you will have the same prints in several colors; and you may not be able to find some colors at all. Instead of settling for "instant scraps," set out to build up you stash over a period of time, buying when you see something you like, or buying to fill gaps in your collection. Eventually, you will have a fabric collection with depth and variety that will make your quilts sing.

BUILDING A GLORIOUS STASH OF FABRICS FOR SCRAP QUILTS

✔ Go on a buying trip when you start a quilt. Replenish fabrics in colors that you will be using before you use them all up.

✔ Buy whenever you see something you love. It won't be around for long.

✔ Buy when you need inspiration. There is nothing like a pile of new fabric to get your creative juices flowing.

✔ Buy when the fabric is on sale. There are always prints that you like but haven't bought before because of the expense. When they are on sale, all of a sudden they look indispensable.

✔ Periodically, make a shopping list of gaps in your collection, and make a special trip to the store just to fill these gaps and round out your collection.

✔ Buy extra fabric whenever you make any project. The leftovers will make a great addition to your stash. (When I am starting a project, I like to buy everything that I might consider including. This way, I don't have to make up my mind until I get home. I never mind having bought something that I didn't use right away. It just goes into my stash. I have been known to buy ten or fifteen yards of fabric to make a single 36" quilt!)

✔ Buy fabric when you are on vacation. People always seem to budget some extra spending money into their vacations. Fabric makes the perfect souvenir: you will always recall your vacation when you see that fabric on your shelf or in your quilts.

✔ Finally, don't spend all of your time shopping. After all, the point is to make quilts, not simply to collect fabric.

You will need to temper these guidelines according to your personal situation. After all, there is no sense buying more fabric than you have space to store or money to pay for. If you can afford it and it gives you pleasure don't worry about having more fabric than you will ever use. A fabric collection by itself is every bit as valid as a baseball card collection or a stamp collection. And it is such a creative energizer!

The amount of fabric that you buy should relate to how much fabric you already have, how much room you have to store it accessibly, how much you can afford, what use you see for it, and how many projects you actually make. My stash is large, while my storage space is dwindling. I usually buy a yard if I adore a fabric, a half yard if I like it and I am looking for inspiration, and a fat quarter if I am desperate for the color now but don't envision using it for later projects. If a fabric is perfect for borders I will buy three yards. I usually buy fabric for background, sashes, or other non-scrap elements after I have a particular project in mind.

Your needs may vary. If you are trying to build a collection from scratch, buy half-yard lengths of as many fabrics as you can afford. Fat quarters will be used up as fast as you buy them if you have a limited amount of fabric. And that is no way to build a collection!

What a delightful idea: buying fabric just to have it! (Most of us have been doing it for years and feeling guilty about it.) You don't have to feel guilty when you buy more than you need or when you don't use it as planned. You are simply building your stash. It feels wonderful when you put your stash to good use making a beautiful Scrap Quilt, and it is so comforting to know that you still have plenty of fabric for the next quilt! (I'm planning on having plenty of fabric for my heirs, as well.)

QUILTMAKING WITH A TODDLER UNDERFOOT

This chapter is dedicated to a student I had many years ago who asked, innocently enough, how I managed to get any quiltmaking done. After I went on about not having a television to distract me, foregoing cooking, even skipping meals altogether, staying up 'til the wee hours, and taking the phone off the hook, she politely inquired, "but what about the children?" I am embarassed to say I brushed off the question, saying something to the effect of "How should I know? I don't have a husband or children." I should have opened the topic to the rest of the class for discussion, instead. You will be pleased to hear that the tables have turned. That student's children are teenagers by now, and they probably want some private time as much as their mother wanted some years ago. I, on the other hand, now have a three-year-old and a one-year-old, and I know exactly what she meant by her question so long ago.

The subject of quiltmaking to the pitter-patter of little feet boils down to two things: childproofing and finding time. If your children nap or go to bed at a reasonable hour, finding time becomes a matter of getting the rest of your work done while the children are up so you can work on your quiltmaking projects while they sleep. I realize that this is not always realistic. My son was the baby who would not sleep. In this case, childproofing becomes all the more important, because you'll have to sew with an inquisitive child underfoot.

CHILDPROOFING FOR A SAFE & SECURE SEWING AREA

Childproofing is more than simply putting latches on the drawers and cupboards. My daughter had busted all of the cabinet latches long before her brother was born. Around our house, my husband and I are driven to comment every two or three weeks, "This is the end of life as we know it." Junior has learned to crawl or to open doors or to climb on chairs or to move a chair to climb to some desired trophy. Things that were safely out of reach just yesterday are fair game today. Of course, you will probably learn of your child's new skill by catching him with a seam ripper in one hand and a loaded pin cushion in the other if you don't change your habits well ahead of your child's development.

Before your child is crawling is the time to begin the practice of hunting for that dropped pin the instant it hits the floor. Don't put it off until you finish your seam. Do it now. And if you don't find it, keep looking until you do. This is also the time to stop leaving your iron, hot or cold, on the ironing board. It doesn't take much of a jostle to knock the iron off the board. My ironing board is right next to my sewing table, which is much wider and more stable. I keep the iron far back on the table, near the wall. If your iron doesn't have a cool base, put a portable pad under it on the table. As a further precaution, don't let your iron's cord dangle. I put a six-outlet power strip on my table top, with only the one cord plugged into the wall outlet. My iron, sewing machine, and lamp are plugged into the power strip. It would take a lot of tugging to dislodge the appliances by pulling on the power strip cord!

When your child begins to creep or crawl, pulling to stand may be just a moment away. This is the time to put your pins in a screw-top container and keep scissors, rotary cutters, seam rippers, and needles in a child-proof box. I have a tin box with a tight lid. It has proven sufficient for me so far, but I have been eyeing a clever box in a children's catalogue. It can only be opened by someone whose finger is long enough to reach through a hole to a latch designed to elude the small and curious. When I am sewing, I keep the pins, scissors, and other necessary tools available to me, but I make a point to keep everything pushed back from the edge of the table, out of reach of toddlers. I do not leave the room for even a moment without putting the tools back in the box, turning off the iron, and pushing the portable sewing machine, along with the foot pedal and cord, far back on the table.

You know your children best. You may need to take more drastic measures to protect your children and your tools. Don't assume your children are safe just because they haven't gotten into anything yet. Maybe a door with a lock will be the only safe course of action. While you have safeguards in mind, don't forget to protect your projects. Of course, you will keep your quilt top out of reach if it has pins in it. But your child can unravel your work in no time or drag it through the cat box, or dip it in cocoa, or strew seven hundred squares and triangles all over the house, or do any number of unimaginable things if you don't protect your project from your children as well as protecting your children from sewing hazards.

THE CHALLENGE: MAKING TIME FOR QUILTMAKING

As for finding time, my best advice is to eliminate the unnecessary. Cut out some of the television time or visiting with neighbors. Streamline meals, serving dishes that cook themselves. A pot of spaghetti or homemade soup cooks for hours and looks impressive, but it doesn't really take much of your time. Furthermore, you can usually get several meals out of one pot. Make your family understand that you need some time to yourself. Each person should be doing his own reasonable share of the work. If you can afford it, consider paying someone to clean your house. If you can't afford it, can you lower your standards a bit while you finish your quilt? You may find that by lowering your standards, you exceed someone else's "dirt threshold," and that person's cleaning instinct kicks in. (Or maybe not.)

All other distractions aside, there is still the matter of the children. I find it helpful to keep a box of quiet toys and books set aside to bring out in my sewing room when I want to keep the children occupied while I sew. If they haven't seen these particular toys for awhile, so much the better. Sometimes, the children just want to be near me. I let them make a mess of my fabric shelves if it will keep them happy for longer than it will take me to clean up after them. Once, before I had children, my brother-in-law showed up to do some urgent repairs on my computer. Unexpectedly, he brought along my two- and four-year old nieces. I had twenty-three hours left to do twenty-four hours of sewing before my appointment with the photographer. I didn't have time to babysit. I didn't have toys to entertain the children. I got out a box of fabric scraps, and plopped it and the girls down on the floor at my feet, and they occupied themselves for hours. I chattered with the girls as I worked. They felt like the center of attention as long as I was there to interact with them, commenting on their activities and going along with their pretend play. And I never even left my sewing machine.

There is no substitute for giving your children the attention they deserve. I find that if I read mine a book two or three times or spend a half hour roughhousing, the children are much less likely to hover and whine. They'll let you know when they want attention. My daughter turns my swivel chair around so she can climb on my lap. It's hard to sew when you are no longer facing the sewing machine, and it's simply a bad idea to sew with a toddler on your lap, so I shut off the machine and take a mini-break. After all, the children are only young for a very short time.

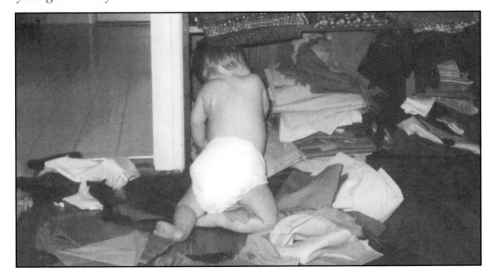

My daughter at age one enjoying my fabric while I sew.

BASIC METHODS &
TIMESAVING TIPS

QUICK SCISSOR CUTTING FOR THE
NOT-QUITE-READY-FOR-ROTARY-CUTTERS CROWD

I realize that some quilters still prefer scissors to rotary tools. Here is a shortcut for scissor cutting that I used for many years. I'm a self-taught quilter who made quilts for years before learning how most people do it. I was astonished to find out that people marked and cut patches one at a time. It never occurred to me to do it that way. My experience had been in dressmaking. When you make clothing, you fold the fabric in half and pin a paper pattern to it. You cut through two layers at a time, without marking. When you sew garments, you guide the edge of the fabric along a seam gauge on the throat plate of the sewing machine, so no seam line markings are necessary.

I based my quiltmaking methods on dressmaking practices. I probably would not be a quiltmaker today if I had had to make that first quilt using time-consuming traditional methods. I'm not that patient. You may enjoy hand work. If so, I respect that. Please feel free to continue to make quilts your own way. However, if you've been longing for a shortcut and you are comfortable with a sewing machine, read on.

If you have ever used a sewing machine to make a simple skirt or dress, you will find this method to be quite natural. The method is quick, accurate, and versatile, as well.

Forget about templates. Instead, you will be using paper patterns (as you do in dressmaking). The paper need not be heavy. In fact, it should be flexible. Deluxe tracing paper or graph paper are ideal. Trace or rule your pattern with seam allowances included. (There is no need to trace the seam lines. The cutting lines will suffice.) Fold your fabric, with selvedges together, on your ironing board. Press the layers together. Fold again to make four layers, if desired. Press again. The layers should be smooth and even. Pin your pattern to the top layer, observing grain lines. One pin is enough for most squares or triangles; a couple of pins will do for longer patches. Don't pin through all the layers. That will make the pattern bow down around the pin and flip up around the edges. It is easier to cut accurately with the pin catching only the top layer. Cut around the pattern through all layers with good, sharp scissors.

Fold and press four layers of fabric. Pin a paper pattern to the top layer with a single pin. Cut around the pattern through all four layers. Use sharp scissors to take vertical strokes at the middle of the blades.

Be careful not to shift the layers of fabric as you cut. Hold the scissors straight, not angled, so that the blades cut through all layers with a vertical stroke. If your scissors are tipped at an angle, patches on the bottom layer may be larger or smaller than ones on the top layer. Use somewhat short strokes, cutting in the middle of the blades rather than at the tip or back. Cutting at the tip makes for little, mincing strokes that are jerky and inefficient. Cutting at the back of the blade lifts the fabric too much and makes it difficult to keep the layers even and the pattern in place.

Be sure to cut off the points of the patches as indicated on the patterns. This will provide clues for positioning patches for machine piecing, and it will reduce bulk in the seam allowances. Cut patches edge to edge, aligning the pattern piece with the edge already cut for the last patch. You don't need too trim off the selvedge, but avoid it when you position your pattern for cutting. The selvedge may shrink disproportionately, causing billows, or it may be printed with the manufacturer's name or have perforations or an unprinted edge that will look like a glaring error if it shows up in your quilt. It is best simply to steer clear of the selvedge.

If your pattern gets dog-eared, make a new one. Cut the largest patches first; smaller patches can be cut from the leftovers.

If you are cutting symmetrical patches, such as squares, diamonds, rectangles, isosceles triangles (having two sides the same length), kites, octagons, arrows, or trapezoids, you can turn the pattern over after you cut each stack of four. The pattern will curl up as you cut, and by turning it over, you can flatten it again.

Occasionally, a pattern calls for asymmetrical patches (ones that are different when viewed from the back). A rhombus (a right triangle stuck on the end of a square or rectangle), a parallelogram (a diamond with two longer sides), or a long, pointy triangle with sides of three different lengths is asymmetrical. When a pattern in this book calls for an asymmetrical patch as well as its reverse, the reverse is indicated with an "r" after the patch letter. If you need to cut patches and their reverses in equal numbers (that is, if you need as many C's as Cr's), you can follow the usual layer-cutting procedure, described above. If you need to cut asymmetrical patches in different quantities or without their reverses, you must unfold the fabric. Cut one patch at a time, being careful to keep the patch right side up as you cut each patch. If you need to cut the same asymmetrical shape from several fabrics, you can layer the different materials, keeping each right side up.

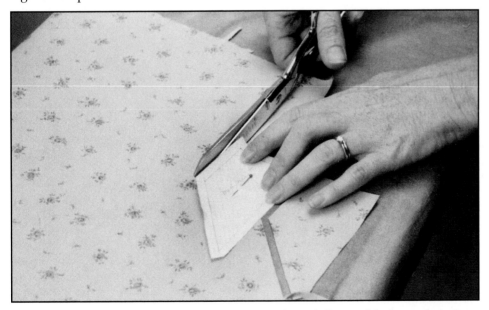

To cut asymmetrical patches and their reverses in equal numbers, cut through four layers of folded fabric, as usual. To cut asymmetrical patches without their reverses, do not fold the fabric. Cut one patch at a time or cut off lengths of fabric and layer them, all right side up. Don't turn the pattern over as you cut these shapes.

To scissor cut Scrap Quilts, you can layer four different fabrics, rather than folding a single fabric into layers. Put fabrics requiring careful alignment, such as stripes and plaids, on the top layers. If you need to cut asymmetrical patches and their reverses for a Scrap Quilt, lay half of the fabrics face up and half face down.

That is all there is to scissor cutting. No marking is needed. In fact, no pinning is needed, either. As you gain experience, you will find that you can simply hold the pattern in place with your fingers without pinning. As you cut, move your fingers as needed to keep the pattern in place. If the pattern gets jostled, simply reposition it.

SETTING UP AN ACCURATE SEAM GAUGE

There are three keys to precise patchwork. The first is an accurate pattern. You have chosen the right book for that. I have drafted the patterns with computer perfection and personally tested each patch by sewing the quilts myself. The second key is accurate cutting. Simply cut your fabric patches to exactly match the patterns. The final key is accurate sewing, which boils down to following an accurate seam gauge. This is where most quilters who have problems get into trouble.

Once, I took my sewing machine to a friend's house to help her make Log Cabin drink coasters for a crafts fair. She had already cut out the strips. We set up our sewing machines at opposite ends of the kitchen table and started working. We got involved in conversation, and the hours passed before we knew it. At some point in the proceedings, one of us stopped working long enough to survey the growing pile of coasters. We seemed to have a problem: My blocks were a half inch larger than hers! How could that be? Different ideas of a ¼" seam allowance was the trouble, it seems. I was using a tape marker and she was using the edge of her presser foot as a guide. The difference in our seam gauges was only slight, but the difference in the completed blocks was quite noticeable. We were lucky. Log Cabin blocks are pretty forgiving, and we were able to make use of all of the coasters (in sets of two sizes), after all. We realized, though, that had we been making some other pattern, we could have had a mess on our hands. Real problems arise when different people with different seam allowances are making blocks for a group quilt, and the blocks turn out different sizes. An individual can also have trouble within a single block if her seam gauge is inaccurate. When one part of a block has more seam allowances than another part, your seams need to be exactly ¼" or the various parts of the block will not fit together.

Check your seam gauge right now. You may be surprised to find that your seam allowances are not exactly ¼" deep, especially if you have been using the edge of your presser foot as a guide. Here is how to correct the problem:

If you have a zig-zag machine, you may be able to adjust your needle position to make perfect ¼" seams using the presser foot as a guide. Simply cut a piece of graph paper with markings at ¼" intervals along one of the lines. Insert the paper under the presser foot, aligning the cut edge with the edge of the presser foot. Adjust the needle until it aligns perfectly with the line that is ¼" from the cut edge. (If you don't have graph paper at hand, trace a pattern from the book, including both seam lines and cutting lines. Cut it out, and align the needle with the seam line and the the presser foot with the cut edge.)

If you can't adjust your needle, you can insert the graph paper or pattern piece under the needle, lower the presser foot, and stitch on the ¼" line or on the seam line for several inches to make sure it is feeding straight. With the paper or pattern still in place and the presser foot still down, put a piece of masking tape on the throat plate of the machine right along the cutting line of the pattern. Use the edge of the tape, rather than your presser foot, as a seam gauge.

To make a precise ¼" seam gauge, machine stitch a few inches along the line that is ¼" from the cut edge of a piece of graph paper or a paper pattern. Before removing the paper, put a strip of masking tape on the throatplate of the machine, following the cut edge of the paper.

SPEEDY MACHINE PIECING

Years ago, when both of us were still fledgling quilters, Marsha McCloskey and I got together to share techniques and ideas. (We still do.) I showed her how I drafted paper patterns and cut them out without marking. She suggested an improvement: cutting out on the ironing board. (This was a real back saver after I had been cutting out on the floor. Now, nearly twenty years later, my back and I are even more grateful to Marsha for the tip.) I introduced Marsha to a seam ripper (We all make mistakes from time to time.), and I showed her how to cut off points to align the patches properly for piecing.

It was Marsha who told me about chain piecing. She described sewing one pair of patches together and then, without stopping to lift the presser foot, continuing right on stitching the next pair of patches. She said that her young daughter, Amanda, (now grown!) would ready the pairs of patches and hand them to her. Marsha raved about the method, but I am afraid that I resisted chain piecing for awhile because I didn't have anyone to help me get the next pair of patches ready. I'm embarrassed to say that it didn't occur to me that I could lift my foot off the pedal and pause to get the next pair of patches ready to sew myself.

Once I tried chain piecing, I was sold on it. You can sew as fast or as slowly as you like. The great advantage is that you avoid all those nasty thread ends and snarly knots that come with starting and stopping in the usual way. You can save a great deal of thread (and bobbin winding), and you can avoid the tedious snipping of threads on the back of your quilt. (I always hated snipping those threads. I would take the last seam, and instead of rejoicing at finishing my quilt, I got to look forward to another hour of anticlimactic thread snipping.)

EFFICIENT, EFFORTLESS CHAIN PIECING

Join two patches in a seam, stitching from edge to edge of the patches and backtacking at both ends. Come to a stop, but leave the presser foot down. Prepare the next pair of patches. Slip the next pair of patches under the tip of the presser foot (without lifting it). Stitch through thin air for a couple of stitches until the second pair of patches reaches the needle. Stitch the second pair of patches together, backtacking at both ends. The first pair of patches will be attached to the second by a twist of thread. Continue joining patches in pairs. Snip the threads between pairs when you are ready to go on to the next step. Sometimes, it is handy to keep all of the units or some of the units chained together until you are ready to use them in another step. For example, when I am making a Scrap Quilt with several patches of the same fabric in one block, I make the units having matching fabric in succession. Then when I snip the units apart, I leave the matching units chained together until I am ready to use them in a later step.

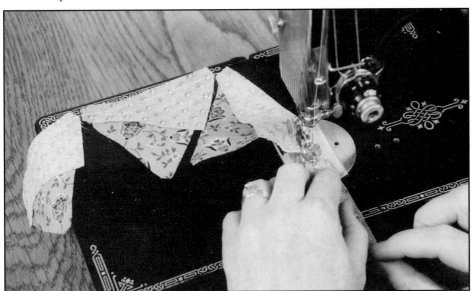

To chain piece, make a seam. Leave the presser foot down. Slip the next pair of patches under the tip of the presser foot. Sew through thin air for a couple of stitches, then sew the seam, again leaving the presser foot down. Snip threads between pairs of patches before going on to the next step.

Some machines balk at stitching right up to the edge of the fabric. They may push the fabric down the hole or make a huge knot on the bobbin side. This is not usually a problem with chain piecing. With no long thread tails to tangle, the stitching proceeds more smoothly. I have found that it is also helpful to avoid stitching over the edge of the fabric in reverse. I make it a point to start and end each seam on a forward stitch. I stop about one stitch shy of the edge when I backtack, and I never have problems with snarls and tangles. For the same reason, I also make it a point to stitch from the square end of a triangle toward the pointed end whenever possible. Occasionally, the pointed end can get pushed down the hole with the needle if you start your line of stitching there.

THE ASSEMBLY-LINE ADVANTAGE

Assembly-line strategies go hand-in-hand with chain piecing. With this approach, you repeat a step for the entire quilt before going on to the next step. For example, you might sew all of the A patches to all of the B patches for the whole quilt before adding a C patch to each. Every pattern in this book is presented with step-by-step instructions that apply chain piecing and assembly-line methods specifically to that pattern. Assembly-line methods mean you only have to think once, and then simply repeat the motion. When you make a whole block before starting the next one, you must rethink each step for each block. The one posssible drawback of assembly-line piecing is that if you make a mistake, you can repeat it dozens, perhaps hundreds, of times before you notice the problem. Therefore, it is important that you compare your unit carefully to the one illustrated in the pattern instructions before repeating each step.

OPPOSING SEAMS FOR FLAWLESS JOINTS

Generally, in patchwork, seam allowances are pressed to one side rather than being pressed open. This keeps the batting from seeping through the spaces between the stitches. It also forms ridges that will help you align seams perfectly at joints. Here is how:

When you are preparing to stitch across a joint, finger-press the seam allowances in opposite directions. Hold the joint between your thumb and forefinger and slide the two halves until they stop at the ridge formed by the seam allowances. At this point, the joint matches perfectly. Stick a pin in at an angle across both sets of seam allowances, and stitch.

For a perfect joint, oppose seams, finger-pressing them in opposite directions. Pin the joint at an angle to hold down seam allowances on both sides of the joint, and stitch.

Wherever possible, turn the unit so that you are stitching across the seam allowance on the top side before you stitch across the seam allowance on the bottom side. This prevents the unseen, bottom seam allowance from misbehaving, since it is turned the way the feed dogs force it, anyway.

The instructions for each pattern in this book include directions for pressing seam allowances so that they will oppose for perfect joints. If you find that you have stitched across a seam allowance turned the wrong way, it is not necessary to rip out the entire seam. Simply release the stitches for the ¼" or ½" in question, turn the seam allowances properly, and restitch. Backtack and blend the new segment of the seam into the original seam.

If you accidentally stitch a seam with the seam allowances turned the wrong way, don't rip out the whole seam. Use a seam ripper to undo only the few stitches across the seam allowances. Then pin and stitch again, backtacking to secure the ends of the seam.

PRESSING PERFECTION

It is important to press each fabric thoroughly before cutting patches from it. All-cotton fabrics sometimes are marbled with small wrinkles after preshrinking. You won't have the opportunity to press out the wrinkles after you have cut out patches, so be sure to do that before you begin. Dampen the fabric or use steam to get out every last wrinkle. For stubborn wrinkles, sometimes a light spray of starch helps. After you have cut out the patches, take care not to rumple the fabric too much with handling.

As you join the patches together, crease the seams to one side using your thumbnail rather than using an iron. I lay the unit on my thigh, with patches face to face and wrong sides out, as for stitching. The patch toward which I will be pressing the seam allowances is on top. I then flip the top patch over so that I am looking at the right side of the unit, opened flat. I run my thumbnail along the seam line to train the seam allowance in the right direction. This is called finger-pressing. Pressing with an iron can stretch bias edges at this stage, and it should be avoided until only straight edges remain unstitched. I press my fabric before cutting patches, and I usually don't press with an iron again until the blocks are complete. Careful finger-pressing prevents unsightly tucks and preserves the ridges of the joints (which an iron can obliterate) to make perfectly matched joints a breeze.

Finger-press seams to preserve the ridges that help you oppose seams for perfect joints. Turn the seam allowances to one side, and run your thumbnail along the seam line.

JOINING BLOCKS INTO A QUILT TOP

For quilts having blocks set side by side, sew the blocks together edge to edge to make straight rows. You will need to oppose seam allowances and pin at each joint. Then join the rows of blocks edge to edge, again opposing seams and pinning joints.

For sashed sets, sew one sashing strip between each two blocks. Make whole rows of blocks alternating with sashes. An extra sash may or may not be sewn to each end of each row, depending on the quilt design. Also make sash rows by joining sashes end to end with setting squares between them. Add a setting square at each end if your block rows end with sashes. Join block rows with sash rows between them. An extra sash row may or may not be sewn to each end of the quilt, depending on the design.

For alternate block sets, you will alternate pieced blocks and plain squares or two different pieced blocks to make a row. Odd-numbered rows start and end with one kind of block; even-numbered rows start and end with the other block. Join rows in sequence to complete the quilt top.

In a diagonal set, the rows run from corner to corner of the quilt, rather than from side to side. Individual rows for a diagonally set quilt look just like rows for a straight set, with blocks joined edge to edge, except that each row ends with two large triangles. Wheareas rows are all the same length in a straight-set quilt, the rows vary in length in a diagonally set quilt.

In order to sew blocks side by side in a diagonal set, arrange the blocks on the floor, placing each at an angle with the corners of the blocks at the top, bottom, and sides of the quilt. Notice how the blocks are in rows that run diagonally across the quilt. Join blocks edge to edge, with the first row (at one corner of the quilt) having just one block. The second row has three blocks sewn edge to edge. The third row has five blocks, and so on, with each row progressively longer. Rows taper again, getting shorter and shorter, as you approach the opposite corner of the quilt. When you have your blocks arranged on the floor, you can spread the blocks apart between rows before sewing them. This will help you see the rows. In order to square off the edges of the quilt, you will need to add large triangles. Sew these triangles to the ends of the rows before joining rows.

Diagonal sets can also include sashes or alternate blocks. Individual rows are made just as you would make them for a straight set, with blocks' edges sewn to sashes or alternate blocks. Lay out the blocks and the other patches on the floor, being sure to include the edge and corner triangles. Spread the blocks and patches into diagonal rows to see how to sew them together.

ADDING BORDERS TO FRAME YOUR QUILT

Once your quilt top is assembled, you are ready to add borders. These can be abutted or mitered. Butting is easier, and it usually takes a little less fabric than mitering. To abut borders, sew a strip to one long side of the quilt, and trim the ends square, even with the edges of the quilt. Repeat for the opposite side. Then sew borders to the top and bottom of the quilt, trimming the ends even with the sides of the bordered quilt.

To miter borders, cut the strips a little longer than the finished quilt dimensions, including borders. Fold a border strip in half crosswise to find the center. Match this point to the center of the side of the quilt, and pin. Pin, then stitch the border to the quilt top, stopping and backtacking ¼" from the ends of the quilt top. Repeat for the other three sides. With your border face down, use your rotary ruler to mark a line at a 45° angle from the end of the seam line to the corner of the border. Lay the ¼" line of your rotary ruler on this line and cut ¼" outside the marked line. Repeat for all eight border ends. Stitch a short seam at each border corner. Start exactly at the end of the seam line joining borders to the quilt top, and proceed along the marked line to the corner of the quilt.

TRICKS OF THE TRADE

✔ Make sure that your sewing machine is outfitted with a number eleven (broadcloth) needle. Anything lighter may be too fragile. Anything heavier may make unnecessarily large holes. Change the needle at the first sign of a burr. Needles are inexpensive, and a burred one can pull the threads of your fabric and ruin your quilt.

✔ Choose a neutral thread color. I usually use beige. It is not necessary to change thread to match the fabric for every seam. If you are concerned about the stitches showing, match the thread to the fabric toward which you will be pressing the seam allowances. If you have a number of bobbins wound ahead of time, some with dark thread and others with light, it is a simple matter to pop in a different bobbin when you are going to be stitching on a border or sewing a whole slew of assembly-line patches the same color. You can usually leave your beige thread on the top and stitch patches with a dark bobbin and the dark patch down.

✔ Opinions vary on stitch length. I feel that 10 stitches per inch makes a perfect seam. A shorter stitch makes an unnaturally firm seam that is difficult to rip out in case of error. A longer stitch is too much like a gathering stitch.

✔ Pin long seams at intervals of about four inches. Pin at each joint to be matched, and pin borders at intervals of about four to six inches. It is not necessary to pin seams shorter than about fifteen inches when no joints need to be matched.

✔ If your cutting and sewing are accurate, there should be no need to fudge. However, if you should ever need to ease one side of a seam slightly, stitch it with the full side down. The machine will take up the slack for you.

✔ Be consistent when joining patches assembly-line style. Always stitch patches with the same lead edge and the same patch on top. This way, you will avoid careless mistakes.

✔ When seam allowances cannot be opposed at a joint, pin right next to the joint on the side without the seam allowances. (That is, pin in the ditch.) Stitch right up to the pin, but remove it rather than stitching over it.

✔ When you have stitched a seam and there is a gap at a joint, release the seam for an inch or two. Instead of putting one pin through the joint, use two pins, right next to the joint on each side. Stitch the seam again, stitching over the pins. If after a couple of tries a joint still slips, try pressing seam allowances contrary to the way you want them. When you turn the seams back again there should be more of a ridge to keep the joint aligned.

✔ If your machine will stitch over pins without balking, use very fine, small silk pins. That way, your stitching will not waver at the pins.

✔ Support the weight of the fabric when pinning long seams. Don't let your quilt droop and stretch out of shape.

✔ When the lower tension gets out of adjustment, before touching the tension knob, remove the throat plate of the machine and brush out the lint. Also brush lint from around the bobbin case area. Check the stitching again; it may no longer need adjustment.

✔ When sewing a Scrap Quilt, sew first those patches that you think will be most difficult to pair with other fabrics. You will have the whole range of partners to choose from. When there are just a half dozen patches left to join at any stage, pair all of the remaining patches before sewing any. This will allow you to make more attractive pairings than might be possible if you just let the piles run down to the last patch before thinking about how they will look together.

THE GRAND FINALE: QUILTING AND BINDING

Once you have completed your quilt top and added the desired borders, you will want to give it one last, good pressing with an iron. Pick off or snip any stray threads. Search for forgotten pins in the seams. Now, if you haven't already planned it, it is time to think about the quilting. There are four basic kinds of quilting, as follows:

✔ In-the-Ditch Quilting. This quilting is directly beside the seam lines on the side without the seam allowances. In-the-ditch quilting is done "by eye," without marking. It can be a little tough to manipulate the fabric onto the needle so close to bulky seam allowances, and you will have to cross over seam allowances at joints. This makes it a little harder to make perfect stitches when you are quilting in the ditch, but being so close to the seam lines, the stitches tend to be barely visible, so any irregularity or unevenness is minimized. One very real advantage is that quilting in the ditch reduces the amount of quilting to about half that needed for outline quilting.

✔ Outline Quilting. This also follows the seam lines. However, it is done ¼" from the seams, just beyond the seam allowances. Since outline quilting is done around each patch, there are two lines of quilting for each seam, one on each side of it. This makes for more quilting. However, you won't need to cross any bulky seam allowances, and the stitching is a little faster and easier. Outline quilting shows up much better than in-the-ditch quilting, so you will want to have small, even stitches. Outline quilting can be done "by eye" or along the edge of ¼"-wide masking tape placed beside the seam. It is not necessary to mark the quilt before basting; simply lay down the tape, one strip at a time, as you quilt in the hoop or frame. To proceed from quilting one patch to another, pass the needle into the batting for ½" and bring it up in the neighboring patch to start quilting there.

✔ Marked Motifs. Alternate plain blocks, borders, sashes, and large patches are often decorated with marked motifs that run the gamut from simple to elaborate. Feathers, cables, and flowers are among the favorites. Marking the motifs takes some care, but quilting them is easy, and the results are splendid. Mark these motifs after pressing the quilt top but before you baste the quilt top to the batting and lining. To do this, you can position a slotted stencil over the quilt and lightly pencil through the slots, or you can position the quilt over a black-marker drawing of the motif and trace onto the quilt top lightly with a pencil. Special quilt marking tools are available at quilt stores. Some wash out, some brush off, and some show up on dark fabrics. Every method has advantages and drawbacks. Ask about these at your local quilt shop, or ask a quilter whose work you admire what tools she uses.

✔ Filler Quilting. Background patterns of parallel lines, grids of squares, or random stippling are used to fill in areas around more fanciful motifs. They serve to depress the surrounding area, making the more important motifs puff up. Straight lines can be marked with masking tape as you quilt. Stippling is random and needs no marking. Filler quilting is time-consuming, but it adds a finished look to a quilt. In times past, when cotton batting required close quilting to stay put, filler quilting was the rule. Nowadays, quilters often forgo it, since polyester batts don't need to be so firmly anchored. Still, some of the best quilts being made today boast fine filler quilting.

Right, in-the-ditch quilting is done right beside the seam, on the side without the seam allowances.

Far right, outline quilting is done ¼" from the seam line, to avoid the seam allowances. You will have two lines of stitching ½" apart flanking each seam.

Right, marked quilting can be used to decorate the larger patches and borders. These are designs that you trace or stencil onto your quilt for stitching.

Far right, filler quilting is done to make the surrounding patches or marked quilting puff out from the background. Straight lines are marked with masking tape. Stippling is very close quilting in an unmarked, random pattern.

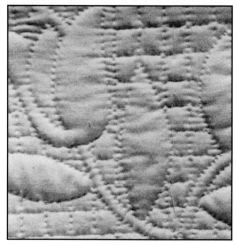

In-the-ditch, outline, marked, and filler quilting can be done by hand or machine, as you prefer. Machine quilting, once shunned by purists is now widely accepted and appreciated. I cannot adequately cover the technique in a page or two. Whole books have been written on the subject. (Harriet Hargrave's

Heirloom Machine Quilting is a good one. Hari Walner's "Continuous Line Quilting Designs" are excellent patterns for machine quilting, and each set includes a pamphlet on machine quilting techniques. Ask for these at your favorite quilting supply source.)

Hand quilting is unquestionably time-consuming. It is also awe-inspiring. The time spent hand quilting is evident to all who see your quilt. A quilt can be rotary cut and machine pieced, but it will still look completely hand made, just like the antique quilts, if you simply quilt it by hand. This is a relaxing activity that you can enjoy while you socialize with friends or family. Hand quilting instructions follow.

Start by preparing the layers. Make a lining 4" longer and 4" wider than your quilt top. Trim off the selvedges and seam together lengths of fabric in a ¼" seam as required for this. Press the lining, pressing seam allowances to one side. Also give the quilt top one last, good pressing. Lay the lining face down on the floor, on a ping-pong table, or on another suitably large surface. Smooth the batting over the lining, trimming the excess batting roughly even with the lining. Center the quilt top, face up, over the batting. Baste the layers together with inch-long stitches in lines four to six inches apart. Mount the quilt in a hoop or frame. It need not be drum-tight, but it shouldn't be entirely slack, either.

Now you are ready to begin quilting. If you have never watched an experienced quilter at work, try to arrange to do so. Many beginners are surprised when they first observe the technique. It helps to see someone doing it comfortably, especially since it may feel totally unnatural to you at first. By watching an experienced quilter you will also have some idea of what stitch length is appropriate. The finest quilters today and in the past have managed perfect, even stitches, 15 to 20 to the inch, counting stitches on the face of the quilt only. Many quilters are satisfied with six or eight stitches to the inch. I think that most contemporary quilters aim for 10 to 15 stitches per inch now. Of course, your stitches may be longer than you would like at first, but they will improve with time and practice. What is most important at first is using the proper technique. Without that, your quilting may never improve.

A self-taught quilter once did a small quilting project for me. It was obvious that she took pride in her work. Her stitches were perfectly even, but they were ¼" long and ¼" apart. I asked her to demonstrate how she quilted. She produced a long needle, which she held between her thumb and forefinger, and proceeded to stitch as if she were basting. When I showed her a few pointers and gave her a #10 betweens needle, she was able to quilt 10 stitches per inch right away. It may not be quite that easy for you, but do try the proper technique.

Cut off a 24" to 36" length of quilting thread. Thread a short needle (#8-12 betweens) with it. The thread should be a single strand with no knot. Take a stitch along the marked quilting line or seam line. Pull the thread to its halfway point, leaving a 12" or 18" tail free. Take short running stitches through all layers. The stitches should be the same length on the top and bottom surfaces of the quilt. Do not grasp the needle between your thumb and index finger; instead, push the needle from the eye end with a thimble on your middle finger. If you are right handed, use your left thumb and middle finger below the quilt to help guide the fabric onto the needle.

Quilt with short running stitches through the layered and basted quilt top, batting, and lining. Use a thimble to push the needle from the end while you depress the fabric in front of the needle with your thumb.

This will probably feel awkward at first, especially if you are not accustomed to using a thimble. However, it is worth getting used to this method, since your fingers will get painfully sore without a thimble, and you will have difficulty achieving the desired short, even stitches unless you rock the needle from the end in this way.

When you reach the end of the thread, take a small backstitch. Then run the needle through the batting to a nearby seam line and take a small stitch right in the valley of the seam line; it will not be visible. Run the thread back in the opposite direction, along the seam line and between layers, for an inch or so. Bring the needle back out. Snip the thread directly at the surface of the quilt top and let the thread end slip back between the layers. Thread the remaining half of the first length of thread into the needle, and continue quilting.

When the quilting is completed, trim the lining and batting exactly even with the quilt top. Remove the basting stitches.

Here is a method for making a double-thick binding: Cut a straight binding strip for each side of the quilt, with strips 1½" wide and about two inches longer than the corresponding edge of the quilt. Press each strip in half lengthwise with right sides out.

Pin a binding strip to one edge of the quilt, with both long raw edges of the doubled binding strip even with raw edges of the quilt top, batting, and lining.

Press the binding strip in half with right sides out and the two long edges together. Pin the doubled strip to the quilt, aligning the cut edges of the binding with the trimmed edges of the quilt.

Trim off the excess length of the binding ¼" beyond the raw edge of the quilt top and turn under the extra at both ends. Stitch through all layers in a ¼" seam. Roll the binding to the back side. Pin, aligning the fold of the binding with the line of stitching just sewn.

After stitching through all layers in a ¼" seam, turn the binding to the back side of the quilt. Pin and hand stitch with the fold of the binding touching the machine stitched seam that you just completed.

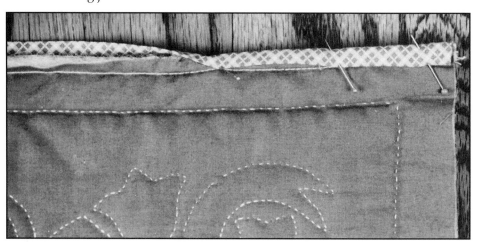

Blindstitch by hand. Repeat for the opposite edge. For the last two edges, turn under the ends of the binding strips to be even with the binding already sewn. Stitch and roll, as before. If desired, you can turn under the excess at an angle for these last two strips to simulate a mitered corner. Embroider your name and the date as a perfect finishing touch.

Heart & Home, 1992, 71" x 93½", designed and made by Judy Martin. Appealing heart blocks are fashioned from the same patches as the neighboring Log Cabins to make this quilt both traditional looking and memorable. The pattern begins on page 51.

Katherine's Bouquet, 1992, 75¾" x 96¼", designed and made by Judy Martin. Inspired by the wealth of pieced flower patterns handed down to us by our quilting forebears, this quilt takes tradition into the 1990's with a pattern that was designed specifically for modern rotary cutting shortcuts. The pattern begins on page 57.

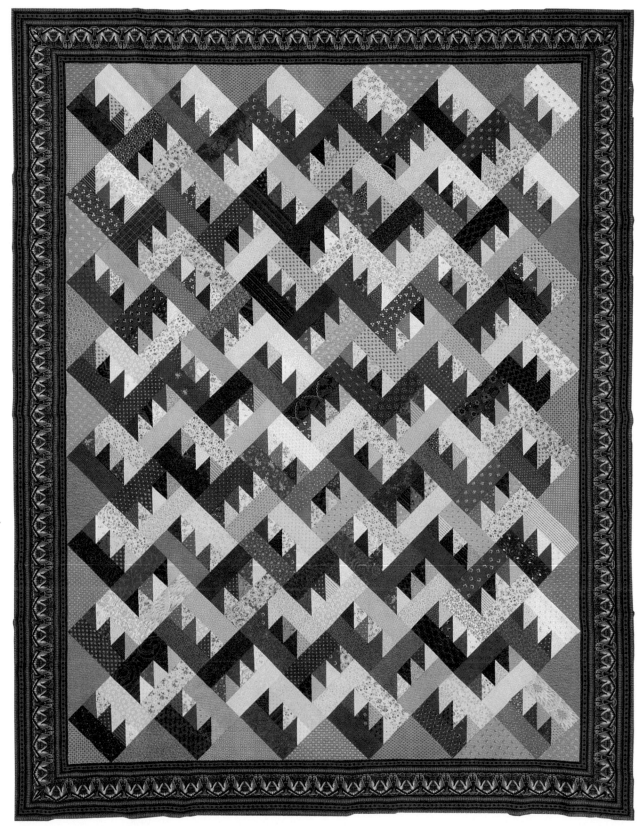

Picket Fence, 1991, 62" x 79", designed and made by Judy Martin. The ever-popular Rail Fence is dressed up here with feathered edges for a simple, yet stunning, new look. Grand patterns, such as intricate star medallions, have long been made even more elegant with the addition of sawtooth triangles. Why not add the same special touch to the most basic pattern? The sawtooths themselves are not difficult, and by adding them to an already easy pattern, you get elegance without aggravation. The pattern begins on page 62.

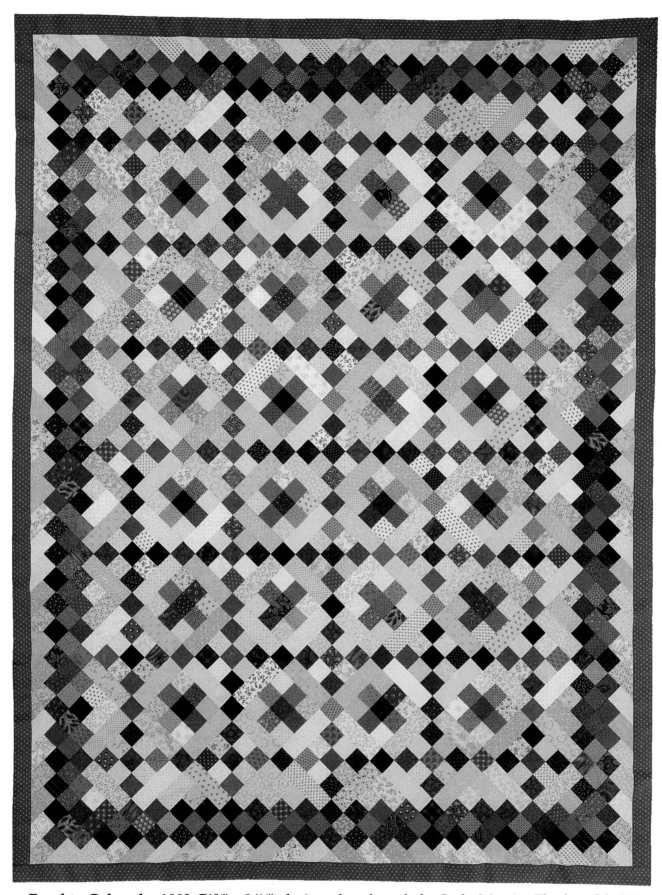

Road to Colorado, 1992, 71⅞" x 94½", designed and made by Judy Martin. The humble Nine-Patch block, set with sashes, is the basis for this masterfully self-bordered, delightfully scrappy confection. The pattern begins on page 66.

Virginia Pinwheel, 1991, 80" x 104", designed and made by Judy Martin. The simple Pinwheel and the venerable Virginia Reel dance magically together in this swirling tribute to the Scrap Quilt. The simplified, side-by-side arrangement of blocks makes it easy to add a third color for a complete change of rhythm. The pattern begins on page 71.

William's Star & Cross, 1992, 71½" x 86¼", designed and made by Judy Martin. A simple combination of scrappy stars and interrupted lattices looks puzzlingly complex. In fact, this pattern is more easily made than an ordinary star and sash. The pattern begins on page 75.

Summerfest, 1992, 70" x 84", designed and made by Judy Martin. The look of an antique Dresden Plate quilt is accomplished here with easy piecing, rather than appliqué. The randomly scrappy block is a simplification of the old-fashioned Sister's Choice pattern. A multicolored sawtooth border completes the traditional impression. This quilt fairly flies together. You'll enjoy making Summerfest so much that you may be tempted to make it over and over again. The pattern begins on page 79.

Red Sky at Night, 1992, 70" x 90", designed and made by Judy Martin. The ever-popular Trip Around the World quilt is an excellent showcase for pretty sequences of blending and contrasting colors and fabrics. Red Sky at Night improves upon the old pattern by adding the illusion of depth. The resulting design falls into a perfectly framed medallion on a bed. The pattern begins on page 83.

Wind in My Sails, 1992, 59" x 82", designed and made by Judy Martin. Blue-and-white quilts have been favorites of quilters for generations. This handsome quilt with its crisp geometry, draws inspiration from the traditional Young Man's Fancy pattern. The block shapes suggest boats and sails, and the unique sawtooth border undulates in a wave-like fashion for a nautical effect. The pattern begins on page 88.

Wedding Memories, 1991, 77" x 95", designed and made by Judy Martin. I have come back to variations of this pattern many times. Like my Daisy Chain, Tennessee Waltz, and Sweethearts' Star designs before it, Wedding Memories combines easy star blocks and octagon blocks to give the illusion of interlocked rings. In my newest version, the rings are filled with shaded chains, reminiscent of a Double Irish Chain. The pattern begins on page 93.

Old Glory, 1991, 61" x 91", designed and made by Judy Martin. The variations in the background fabrics and the offsetting of the stripes give this quilt an interesting fractured appearance. This is the element of surprise that makes a stunning quilt out of an otherwise orderly and straightforward design. The pattern begins on page 97.

Cobblestones, 1991, 68" x 88", designed and made by Judy Martin. A handsome border stripe and a glowing array of scraps make this incomparably easy quilt distinctive and appealing. The pattern begins on page 101.

Hudson Bay Log Cabin, 1992, 74" x 90", designed and made by Judy Martin. This versatile block can be arranged in all of the wonderful, creative Log Cabin sets. The design has the same clever simplicity of a Log Cabin, but with a new and exciting rhythm and a unique texture. What a joy to make something so totally rooted in tradition, and yet so new. The pattern begins on page 105.

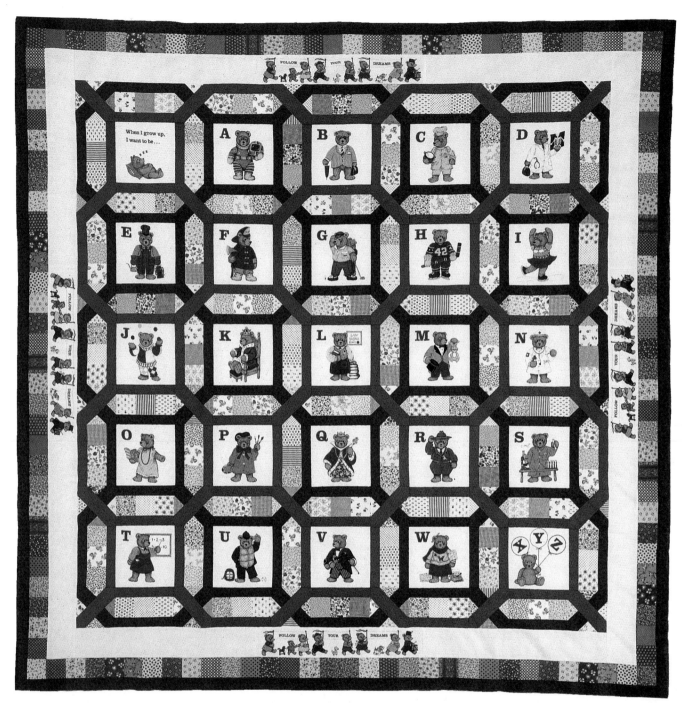

Child's Play, 1991, 66" x 66", designed and made by Judy Martin. Ordinary squares of printed fabric are set in a Garden Maze arrangement with a difference: scrappy patchwork squares punctuate the background and borders. The printed motifs centered in the blocks make a simple pattern special, and the real piecing turns a mass-produced printed panel into a one-of-a-kind treasure. The pattern begins on page 109.

STUNNING COLOR SCHEMES

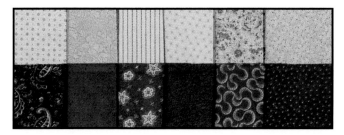

Cream/Red. This is a classic combination for two-color quilts such as Wind in My Sails or Picket Fence. If you like, add a solid accent and use for Hudson Bay Log Cabin.

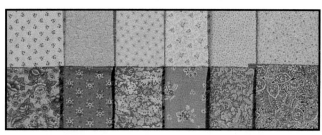

Ivory/Medium Pastel Florals. This is pretty as spring in Wind in My Sails or Picket Fence. Add 1930's green solid accents for Virginia Pinwheel or Hudson Bay Log Cabin.

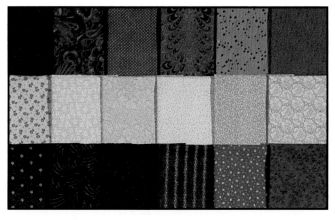

Teal/Tawny Lights/Brown-Black. This is a handsome, old-fashioned color scheme. It would be perfect for Old Glory or William's Star & Cross.

Navy-Blue/Silver-White/Wine/Rose. Here is an elegant assortment of fabrics in blended pairs of colors. Try it in Virginia Pinwheel or Cobblestones.

Red/Blue/Parchment/Brown. This warm variation on a patriotic theme is just the ticket for Cobblestones, Virginia Pinwheel, or Road to Colorado.

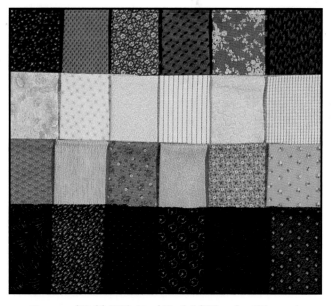

Green/Off-White/Gold/Black. Here is a rich, earthy combination that would give a completely different look to Road to Colorado or Wedding Memories.

MORE COLOR SCHEMES

Fall Shades/Beige. A variety of autumn leaf colors are combined with creamy tones here. The mix is attractive in Heart & Home, Picket Fence, or Child's Play.

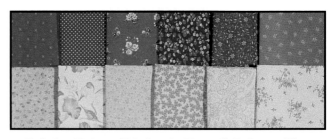

Bright Prints/Light & Pastel Prints. These fabrics look pretty in Picket Fence or Wind in My Sails patterns, or, in combination with a solid accent, in Hudson Bay Log Cabin.

Red/Off-White/Green. Fabulous flower quilts have been made in these colors for generations. Make Katherine's Bouquet in these colors for a most striking quilt.

Multicolored Brights/White/Red-Pink. This lively mix of fabrics makes a perky Heart & Home quilt for someone young or young-at-heart.

Fall Prints/Fall Solids/Tawny/Brown. Try these fabrics in Summerfest, or delete the browns for Wind in My Sails, with the solids used for the small squares and rectangles.

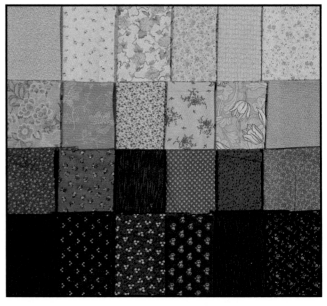

Ivory/Light Pink/Rose/Maroon. These gradated shades make a pleasing Wedding Memories, Road to Colorado, or William's Star & Cross quilt.

SIMPLE PATTERNS

HOW TO USE THESE PATTERNS

The pages that follow are full of helpful instructions, charts, and illustrations. To get the most out of them, read this chapter first. For each quilt in this book, there is a color photograph (pages 33-46), and complete pattern and directions (pages 51-112). Each pattern begins with a brief description including information about the origin of the pattern as well as dimensions for the quilt. Below this descriptive paragraph is a black-and-white drawing of the quilt in one of the sizes not photographed. Beside the quilt drawing is a listing of features that make the quilt an easy one to cut and sew. At the bottom of the introductory page for each pattern are notes regarding my choice of colors and fabrics as well as suggestions for additional color schemes. Many of these color schemes are photographed on pages 47-48. Please feel free to interpret my patterns creatively.

YARDAGE AND CUTTING REQUIREMENTS CHART

On the second page of each pattern, you will find yardage and cutting requirements listed in a chart. Each listed fabric is preceded by a box shaded to match the patches in the quilt drawing and diagrams. Note that, for most quilts, there are three sections to this chart, one for each quilt size. Refer to only that section of the chart that describes the quilt size you are making.

Within the sections, the column listing "No. Pcs." is a suggestion for the number of different fabrics of a given color that would be easy to use in the Short Strips method and would also provide suitable variety for a Scrap Quilt. If you do not want to make a Scrap Quilt, use just one fabric for each color listed. If you have plenty of different fabrics and like a scrappy look, you can use a different fabric for each strip.

The "Tot. Yds." column indicates the yardage needed to cut strips and patches as described for each color from a single 44"-wide fabric. I allowed for 4% shrinkage in my computations. You won't need to know yardage figures for a Scrap Quilt, but the yardage listed will give you an idea of the total required.

The "Patches" column identifies the full-size pattern pieces by letter and lists the quantity needed of each letter. The quilt construction directions refer to these patch letters, as well. If you are using the Rotary Patch technique, the resulting patches will match the full-size patterns, so they are identified by the same letters. Sometimes, strip cutting will yield a few extra patches. Compare your strip-cut totals to the totals here, and set aside the extras to avoid unnecessary sewing.

Dimensions for border and binding strips are listed in the top chart only. Cut border and binding strips before cutting Short Strips and Rotary Patches as listed in the second chart. The yardage for the borders is sufficient to cut matching binding. If you want seamless binding from a contrasting fabric, buy the amount listed in parentheses for binding, as well as the border yardage listed.

AT-A-GLANCE ROTARY CUTTING OF STRIPS AND PATCHES CHART

Below the Yardage And Cutting Requirements Chart is an At-A-Glance Rotary Cutting Chart. This tells how to cut Short Strips and Rotary Patches for each color category in the quilt. The first six columns of this chart apply to all quilt sizes. The last few columns list the number of strips of each type needed for the various quilt sizes.

The first column lists fabrics by color category. You may use a different piece of fabric for each color, if desired.

The second column lists the measurement of the strip on the lengthwise grain. Usually, this is 18" for Short Strips. Sometimes, it is 9" for Mini Strips. Your fabric can be a little shorter than the 18" or 9" listed and still accommodate all the patches listed. I have allowed about ½", sometimes more, for shrinkage from a ½-yard or ¼-yard cut of fabric. Occasionally the Strip Length is longer to accommodate a longer patch. In such cases, you will need to cut the exact length listed.

The third column lists the quantities and measurements of crosswise cuts to each strip. Always start with a clean cut at one end of the strip, at right angles to the long edges. A notation such as "6 @ 2½"" means that you are to measure and cut the strip crosswise 2½" from the clean end, then measure and cut again 2½" from the new edge, and so on until you have cut off six pieces, each measuring 2½". Sometimes, this column will have a notation such as "*C." This means that you will find a detailed description and diagram of the cutting procedure for that patch in the Special Rotary Cutting Instructions.

The "Additional Cuts" column refers you to the Special Cutting Instructions where necessary. Basic triangles are indicated with an icon. Other shapes are listed by patch letter and an asterisk. Once you get used to these references, you will find the icon sufficient to tell you how to cut the patches so indicated.

The "Yield Per Strip" column tells you how many patches of what letters you can cut from a single strip. These numbers are the same for every quilt size.

The last columns list the number of strips of each type needed for each quilt size. If you are using true scraps and fabric remnants that may differ in length from the listed strip length, you may need a different number of strips for your quilt. Refer, instead, to the "Patches" column of the other (Yardage and Cutting Requirements) chart. This will give you a total for each patch. Keep track of the patches you cut from each strip if your strip lengths vary from those listed.

SPECIAL ROTARY CUTTING INSTRUCTIONS

Following the charts are the Special Rotary Cutting Instructions already mentioned. Patches indicated with an asterisk in the At-A-Glance Chart require more than just lengthwise and crosswise cuts. In this section, you will find specific instructions for cutting these patches.

QUILT CONSTRUCTION AND AT-A-GLANCE DIAGRAMS

Directions for Quilt Construction are next. These are broken down into small steps. Steps are numbered to match the unit numbers in the illustrations. Quantities needed for each quilt size are listed by the figures. Refer to pages 7-32 for extra help with basic techniques and new shortcuts. Experienced quiltmakers can simply refer to the At-A-Glance Diagrams and their captions, skipping the narrative altogether. Note that for most of the quilts in this book, you sew the patches into units; then you sew these units to other units or patches to form larger units. For easy reference, I call the resulting blocks "units," as well.

Once you have completed all of the required units, you must assemble them into a quilt top. Here, the directions are usually separate for the various quilt sizes, with headings in bold to make it easy to find reference to your size. A whole quilt diagram is provided where it is helpful. I include basic quilting instructions for each quilt, but I encourage you to embellish your quilting with commercial stencils or other motifs, as you desire.

FULL-SIZE PATTERNS

Finally, the full-size patterns are presented. Each pattern has seam lines (dashed) and cutting lines (solid), as well as an arrow indicating the lengthwise grain. A few patterns were too large to fit on the page. These large patches are diagrammed with grain arrows and dimensions (including seam allowances). Seam lines are not shown for these large patterns. Dimensions are also listed for full-size patches that can be rotary cut with easy measurements. For pointed patches, the dimensions are for the entire side, all the way to the point. Note that these dimensions are for the cutting lines, with seam allowances included.

Some patches are used in the quilt two ways, with the grain on different edges. In these instances, both grain arrows are given and the patch letter is further defined by a number to indicate the grain alignment.

Some patterns are asymmetrical. If you need to cut mirror images, the yardage and cutting chart calls for a patch letter and the same letter followed by an "r." Turn the pattern face down for the reversed pieces.

Patterns are presented with points to correspond to the rotary-cut patches. They also have lines to indicate where to trim the points for easy alignment during machine piecing. It is not necessary to trim the points, but it can be helpful. To trim the points of your rotary-cut patches, see the guidelines on page 16.

HEART & HOME

The Log Cabin has always been an easy pattern. This one is extra special with its charming heart blocks, but it is just as easy to make as an ordinary Log Cabin. The same logs used to make the Log Cabin blocks are rearranged to fashion heart blocks in this unique quilt. The quilt photo is on page 33. The drawing of the large quilt is on page 55. Directions are for a 48½" square wall or baby quilt, a 71" x 93½" quilt for a twin or double bed, and a 93½" x 93½" queen or king size quilt. The two larger quilts are arranged in Barnraising sets. The small quilt below is set as a Straight Furrows.

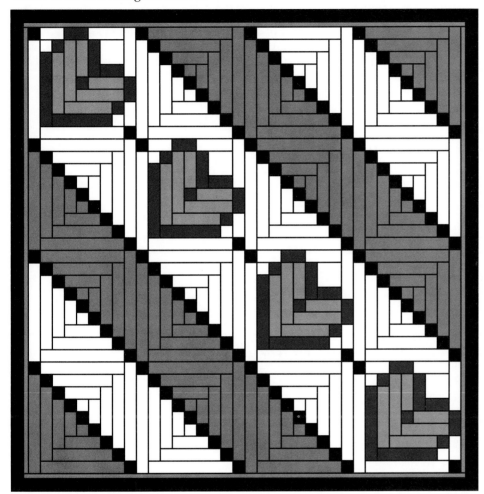

WHAT MAKES THIS QUILT EASY?

✔ Simple squares and rectangles are quick to cut, a breeze to sew. There are no bias edges to stretch out of shape and no points to contend with.

✔ There are very few joints requiring pinning and the little bit of matching is the easiest kind.

✔ Heart & Home has a traditional scale that doesn't skimp on detail, yet it has fewer pieces than most quilts, so the quilt takes less time to make.

I made Heart & Home using a variety of prints in the cream swath, ranging from light pink to white and beige. Although a few standouts were sprinkled in, the medium blue prints were fairly uniform in value to contrast with the single dark blue solid. Rose prints ranged from peachy to pink, with values light enough to contrast with the wine solid.

OTHER STUNNING COLORS

◆ Beige, black, turkey red, and assorted rich, dark shades. For an antique look, choose prints in white, beige, tan, and peach tones to substitute for the cream. Dark prints in brown, green, blue, teal, and red form the other half of the Log Cabin blocks, with black solid squares marching down the center of each block to separate the two halves. Turkey red solid outlines each heart. Lighter reds and bubble-gum pink form the interior of the hearts.

◆ Cream and green Log Cabins with peach hearts.

◆ Parchment and brown Log Cabins with pink hearts.

◆ Butter yellow and blue Log Cabins with purple hearts.

HEART & HOME YARDAGE AND CUTTING REQUIREMENTS

Fabrics	Small - 48½" x 48½" No. Pcs.	Tot. Yds.	Patches	Medium - 71" x 93½" No. Pcs.	Tot. Yds.	Patches	Large - 93½" x 93½" No. Pcs.	Tot. Yds.	Patches
☐ Cream Prints	20	1¼	20 A, 20 B, 16 C, 16 D, 12 E, 12 F, 16 G, 16 H, 4 I	32	3¼	64 A, 64 B, 48 C, 48 D, 32 E, 32 F, 48 G, 48 H, 16 I	44	4¼	84 A, 84 B, 64 C, 64 D, 44 E, 44 F, 64 G, 64 H, 20 I
▨ Blue Prints	24	1	12 A, 12 B, 12 C, 12 D, 12 E, 12 F, 12 G, 12 H	32	2	32 A, 32 B, 32 C, 32 D, 32 E, 32 F, 32 G, 32 H	44	3	44 A, 44 B, 44 C, 44 D, 44 E, 44 F, 44 G, 44 H
■ Dk. Blue Solid (border)	1	1½	116 A 4 @ 1¾" x 49"	1	2⅞	320 A 2 @ 1¾" x 94" 2 @ 1¾" x 71½"	1	2⅞	436 A 4 @ 1¾" x 94"
(binding)		(1½)	4 @ 1½" x 50½"		(2⅞)	2 @ 1½" x 95½" 2 @ 1½" x 73"		(2⅞)	4 @ 1½" x 95½"
▨ Rose Prints	8	½	8 C, 8 D, 8 E	32	1	32 C, 32 D, 32 E	40	1	40 C, 40 D, 40 E
■ Wine Solid	1	½	12 A, 12 B, 4 C, 4 E, 4 F	1	1	48 A, 48 B, 16 C, 16 E, 16 F	1	1	60 A, 60 B, 20 C, 20 E, 20 F
Rose Border	1	1⅜	4 @ 1" x 46½"	1	2¾	2 @ 1" x 91½" 2 @ 1" x 69"	1	2¾	4 @ 1" x 91½"
Lining	1	3⅛	2 @ 27" x 53"	1	5¾	2 @ 38" x 98"	1	8⅝	3 @ 33" x 98"
Batting	1		52½" x 52½"	1		75" x 97½"	1		97½" x 97½"

AT-A-GLANCE ROTARY CUTTING OF STRIPS AND PATCHES

Fabrics	Strip Length	Strip Width	Cross Cuts	Yield Per Strip	Number of Strips Needed Small	Med.	Large
Cream Prints	18"	1¾"	1 @ 3", 1 @ 4¼", 1 @ 9¼"	1 B, 1 C, 1 G	16	48	64
	18"	1¾"	1 @ 5½", 1 @ 10½"	1 D, 1 H	16	48	64
	18"	1¾"	1 @ 1¾", 1 @ 6¾", 1 @ 8"	1 A, 1 E, 1 F	12	32	44
	18"	1¾"	4 @ 1¾", 2 @ 3"	4 A, 2 B	2	8	10
	9"	3"	2 @ 3"	2 I	2	8	10
Blue Prints	18"	1¾"	1 @ 5½", 1 @ 10½"	1 D, 1 H	12	32	44
	18"	1¾"	1 @ 3", 1 @ 4¼", 1 @ 9¼"	1 B, 1 C, 1 G	12	32	44
	18"	1¾"	1 @ 1¾", 1 @ 6¾", 1 @ 8"	1 A, 1 E, 1 F	12	32	44
Dk. Blue Solid	18"	1¾"	10 @ 1¾"	10 A	12	32	44
Rose Prints	18"	1¾"	1 @ 4¼", 1 @ 5½", 1 @ 6¾"	1 C, 1 D, 1 E	8	32	40
Wine Solid	18"	1¾"	1 @ 1¾", 1 @ 6¾", 1 @ 8"	1 A, 1 E, 1 F	4	16	20
	18"	1¾"	2 @ 1¾", 3 @ 3", 1 @ 4¼"	2 A, 3 B, 1 C	4	16	20

AT-A-GLANCE

Unit 1
Make 12 (S),
32 (M), 44 (L).

Unit 2
Make 12 (S),
32 (M), 44 (L).

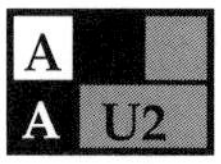

Unit 3
Make 12 (S),
32 (M), 44 (L).

QUILT CONSTRUCTION

Blue/Cream Log Cabin Blocks

1 Sew a dark blue solid A to a blue print A to make Unit 1 as shown. Press seam allowances away from the dark blue solid. Make the quantity indicated for your quilt size.

2 Sew a blue print B to a Unit 1 to make Unit 2 as shown. Press seam allowances away from the Unit 1. Make the quantity indicated.

3 Sew a cream print A to a dark blue solid A. Press seam allowances toward the cream print.

Sew to a Unit 2 to make Unit 3 as shown. Press seam allowances away from the Unit 2. Make the quantity indicated.

4 Sew a cream print B to a dark blue solid A. Press seam allowances toward the cream print. Sew to a Unit 3 to make Unit 4 as shown. Press seam allowances away from the Unit 3. Make the quantity indicated.

5 Sew a blue print C to a Unit 4 to make a Unit 5 as shown. Press seam allowances toward the C patch. Make the quantity indicated.

6 Sew a blue print D to a Unit 5 to make a Unit 6 as shown. Press seam allowances away from the Unit 5. Make the quantity indicated.

7 Sew a cream C to a dark blue solid A. Press seam allowances toward the C patch. Sew to a Unit 6 to make a Unit 7 as shown. Press seam allowances away from the Unit 6. Make the quantity indicated.

8 Sew a cream print D to a dark blue solid A. Press seam allowances away from the A patch. Sew to a Unit 7 to make Unit 8 as shown. Press seam allowances away from the Unit 7. Make the quantity indicated.

9 Sew a blue print E to a Unit 8 to make a Unit 9 as shown. Press seam allowances away from the Unit 8. Make the quantity indicated.

10 Sew a blue print F to a Unit 9 to make a Unit 10 as shown. Press seam allowances away from the Unit 9. Make the quantity indicated.

11 Sew a cream print E to a dark blue solid A. Press seam allowances away from the A patch. Sew to a Unit 10 to make a Unit 11 as shown. Press seam allowances away from the Unit 10. Make the quantity indicated.

12 Sew a cream print F to a dark blue solid A. Press seam allowances away from the A patch. Sew to a Unit 11 to make a Unit 12 as shown. Press seam allowances away from the Unit 11. Make the quantity indicated.

13 Sew a blue print G to a Unit 12 to make Unit 13 as shown. Press seam allowances away from the Unit 12. Make the quantity indicated.

14 Sew a blue print H to a Unit 13 to make Unit 14 as shown. Press seam allowances away from the Unit 13. Make the quantity indicated.

15 Sew a cream print G to a dark blue solid A. Press seam allowances away from the A patch. Sew to a Unit 14 to make Unit 15 as shown. Press seam allowances away from the Unit 14. Make the quantity indicated.

16 Sew a cream print H to a dark blue solid A. Press seam allowances away from the A patch. Sew to a Unit 15 to make Unit 16 as shown. Press seam allowances away from the Unit 15. This completes the Log Cabin Block. Make the quantity indicated.

Unit 4
12 (S), 32 (M), 44 (L).

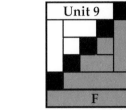

Unit 5
12 (S),
32 (M),
44 (L).

Unit 6
12 (S), 32 (M), 44 (L).

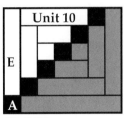

Unit 7
12 (S), 32 (M), 44 (L).

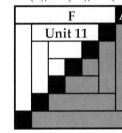

Unit 8
12 (S), 32 (M), 44 (L).

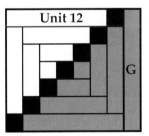

Unit 9
12 (S), 32 (M), 44 (L).

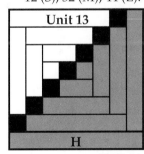

Unit 10
12 (S), 32 (M), 44 (L).

Unit 11
12 (S), 32 (M), 44 (L).

Unit 12
12 (S), 32 (M), 44 (L).

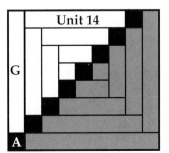

Unit 13
12 (S), 32 (M), 44 (L).

Unit 14
12 (S), 32 (M), 44 (L).

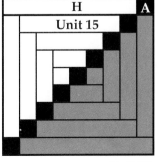

Unit 15
12 (S), 32 (M), 44 (L).

Unit 16
12 (S), 32 (M), 44 (L).

AT-A-GLANCE

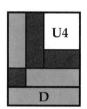

Unit 1
Make 4 (S),
16 (M), 20 (L).

Unit 2
Make 4 (S),
16 (M), 20 (L).

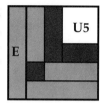

Unit 3
Make 4 (S),
16 (M), 20 (L).

Unit 4
Make 4 (S),
16 (M), 20 (L).

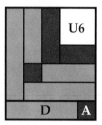

Unit 5
Make 4 (S),
16 (M),
20 (L).

Unit 6
Make 4 (S),
16 (M),
20 (L).

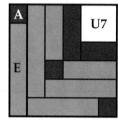

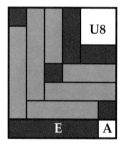

Unit 7
Make 4 (S),
16 (M), 20 (L).

Unit 8
Make 4 (S),
16 (M), 20 (L).

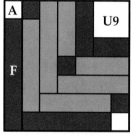

Unit 9
Make 4 (S),
16 (M), 20 (L).

Unit 10
Make 4 (S),
16 (M), 20 (L).

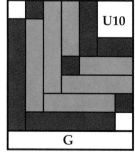

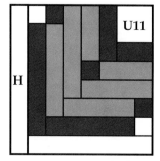

Unit 11
Make 4 (S),
16 (M), 20 (L).

Unit 12
Make 4 (S),
16 (M), 20 (L).

Rose/Cream Heart Blocks

1 Sew a wine solid B to a cream print I to make Unit 1 as shown. Press seam allowances away from the I patch. Make the quantity indicated.

2 Sew a wine solid C to a Unit 1 to make Unit 2 as shown. Press seam allowances away from the Unit 1. Make the quantity indicated.

3 Sew a rose print C to a Unit 2 to make Unit 3 as shown. Press seam allowances away from the Unit 2. Make the quantity indicated.

4 Sew a rose print C to a wine solid A. Press seam allowances away from the A patch. Sew to a Unit 3 to make Unit 4 as shown. Press seam allowances away from the Unit 3. Make the quantity indicated.

5 Sew a rose print D to a Unit 4 to make Unit 5 as shown. Press seam allowances away from the Unit 4. Make the quantity indicated.

6 Sew a rose print E to a Unit 5 to make Unit 6 as shown. Press seam allowances away from the Unit 5. Make the quantity indicated.

7 Sew a rose print D to a wine solid A. Press seam allowances away from the D patch. Sew to a Unit 6 to make a Unit 7 as shown. Press seam allowances away from the Unit 6. Make the quantity indicated.

8 Sew a rose print E to a wine solid A. Press seam allowances away from the E patch. Sew to a Unit 7 to make a Unit 8 as shown. Press seam allowances away from Unit 7. Make the number listed.

9 Sew a wine solid E to a cream print A. Press seam allowances away from the A patch. Sew to a Unit 8 to make Unit 9 as shown. Press seam allowances away from the Unit 8. Make the quantity indicated.

10 Sew a wine solid F to a cream print A. Press seam allowances away from the A patch. Sew to a Unit 9 to make Unit 10 as shown. Press seam allowances away from the Unit 9. Make the quantity indicated.

11 Sew a cream print G to a Unit 10 to make a Unit 11 as shown. Press seam allowances away from the Unit 10. Make the quantity indicated.

12 Sew a cream print H to a Unit 11 to make a Unit 12 as shown. Press seam allowances away from the Unit 11. Make the quantity indicated.

13 Sew a dark blue solid A to a cream print B to a wine solid B to a cream print C. Press seam allowances toward the cream C. Sew to a Unit 12 to make Unit 13 as shown. Press seam allowances away from the Unit 12. Make the quantity indicated.

14 Sew a cream print D to a wine solid B to a cream print B to a dark blue solid A. Press seam allowances toward the cream D. Sew to a Unit 13 to make Unit 14 as shown. Press seam allowances away from the Unit 13. This completes Unit 14, the Heart Block. Make the quantity indicated.

Quilt Assembly

For the small (48½" x 48½") quilt, refer to the diagram on page 51. Arrange 12 Log Cabin Blocks and 4 Heart Blocks in four rows of four blocks each, turning blocks as shown.

For the medium (71" x 93½") quilt, refer to the color photo on page 33. Arrange 32 Log Cabin Blocks and 16 Heart Blocks in eight rows of six blocks each, turning blocks as shown.

For the large (93½" x 93½") quilt, refer to the drawing below. Arrange 44 Log Cabin Blocks and 20 Heart Blocks in eight rows of eight blocks each, turning blocks as shown.

For all sizes, adjust the block placement to achieve a good color balance. Join blocks to make rows. Join rows. Sew a rose border to one side of the quilt. Trim even with edges of blocks. Repeat for the opposite side. Sew another rose border to the top of the quilt. Trim even with the side borders. Repeat for the bottom. Sew a dark blue solid border to one side of the quilt. Trim even with edges of blocks. Repeat for the opposite side. Sew another dark blue solid border to the top of the quilt. Trim even with the side borders. Repeat for the bottom. Join the lining panels. Layer the quilt top, batting, and lining. Baste. Quilt in the ditch around all patches. Bind to finish.

AT-A-GLANCE

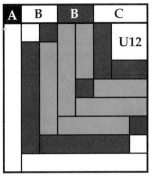

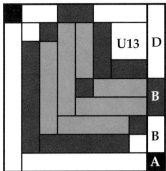

Unit 13
Make 4 (S),
16 (M), 20 (L).

Unit 14
Make 4 (S),
16 (M), 20 (L).

Large Version of Quilt

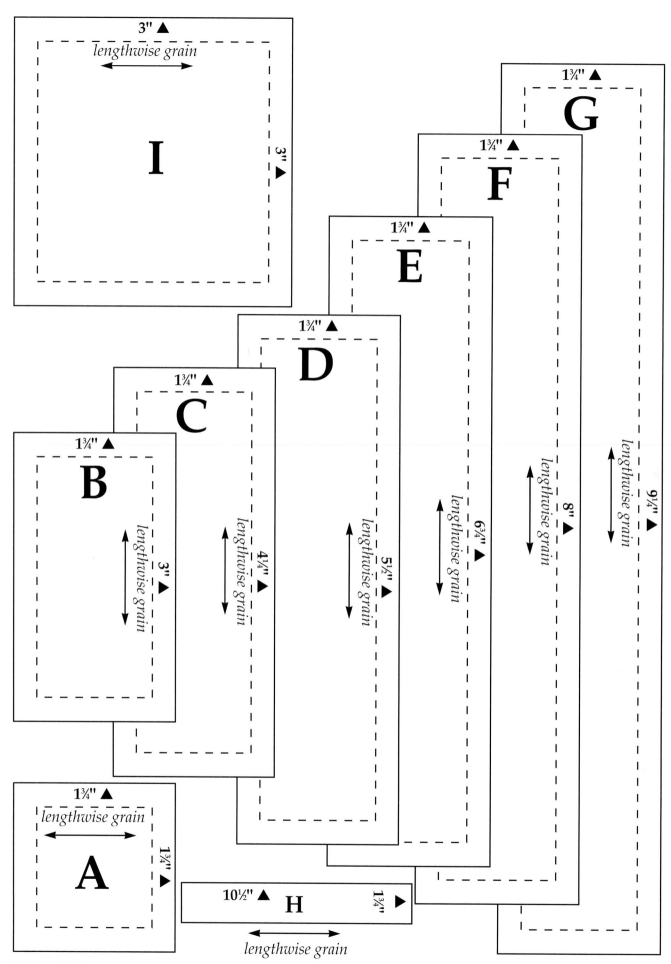

3" ▲
lengthwise grain
3" ▶
I

1¾" ▲
G
lengthwise grain
9¼" ▶

1¾" ▲
F
lengthwise grain
8" ▶

1¾" ▲
E
lengthwise grain
6¾" ▶

1¾" ▲
D
lengthwise grain
5½" ▶

1¾" ▲
C
lengthwise grain
4¼" ▶

1¾" ▲
B
lengthwise grain
3" ▶

1¾" ▲
lengthwise grain
A
1¾" ▶

10½" ▲ **H** 1¾" ▶
lengthwise grain

KATHERINE'S BOUQUET

Katherine's Bouquet is more complex than other quilts in this book, but it is far easier than the traditional patterns it resembles. Pieced flower quilts always look special, and this one is no exception. You won't need exceptional skills to make this flower quilt, however. This one has no set-in patches, no curved or appliquéd stems, and no embroidery. It was designed especially for rotary cutting, with easy-to-measure dimensions and simple shapes. The pattern is presented as a 55¼" square wall quilt (below), a 75¾" x 96¼" twin or double bed coverlet (photo on page 34), and a 96¼" x 96¼" queen or king size quilt.

WHAT MAKES THIS QUILT EASY?

✔ The flower blocks are constructed of simple shapes that can be rotary cut with ease and pieced with straight seams.

✔ The stems are broad for ease of handling and to avoid bulk in the seam allowances.

✔ The wide sashes and diagonal set reduce the number of flower blocks needed, so the quilt can be made relatively quickly.

✔ The flowers are offset from each other to make the seam allowances smoother and to eliminate some matching.

Katherine's Bouquet was made using a single ivory solid for the block backgrounds, a purple print for the edge triangles, a green solid for stems and leaves, and a variety of prints and coordinated, slightly darker solids for the flowers. Red, coral, orange, dark yellow, bright pink, blue, turquoise, and red violet color the blooms in this lively quilt.

OTHER STUNNING COLORS

◆ Red, off-white, and green. This traditional color scheme would make a lovely Katherine's Bouquet either in scraps or just a few fabrics. Substitute unbleached muslin for the block backgrounds, dark green print for stems, your choice of red print or medium green print for the edge triangles, and red prints and solids for the flowers. If desired, make the squares at the base of the flowers a pumpkin solid for accent.

◆ White background; blue triangles; green stems; and red and yellow flowers.

◆ Ivory background; medium rose solid triangles to show off your quilting; mellow green print stems; and dark rose print flowers.

KATHERINE'S BOUQUET YARDAGE AND CUTTING REQUIREMENTS

Fabrics	Small - 55¼" x 55¼" No. Pcs.	Tot. Yds.	Patches	Medium - 75¾" x 96¼" No. Pcs.	Tot. Yds.	Patches	Large - 96¼" x 96¼" No. Pcs.	Tot. Yds.	Patches
☐ Ivory Solid	1	2⅛	30 A, 15 C, 20 D, 5 F, 5 Fr, 10 H, 5 I, 5 Ir, 10 K, 16 M	1	4¼	108 A, 54 C, 72 D, 18 F, 18 Fr, 36 H, 18 I, 18 Ir, 36 K, 48 M	1	5¾	150 A, 75 C, 100 D, 25 F, 25 Fr, 50 H, 25 I, 25 Ir, 50 K, 64 M
(border)			4 @ 3½" x 51¾"			2 @ 3½" x 92¾" 2 @ 3½" x 72¼"			4 @ 3½" x 92¾"
■ Purple Print	1	2¼	10 E$_1$, 20 E$_2$, 10 L, 4 N, 4 O	1	4⅜	36 E$_1$, 72 E$_2$, 36 L, 10 N, 4 O	1	4⅜	50 E$_1$, 100 E$_2$, 50 L, 12 N, 4 O
(border)			4 @ 2½" x 55¾"			2 @ 2½" x 96¾" 2 @ 2½" x 76¼"			4 @ 2½" x 96¾"
(binding)		(1¾)	4 @ 1½" x 57"		(2⅞)	2 @ 1½" x 98" 2 @ 1½" x 78"		(2⅞)	4 @ 1½" x 98"
■ Green Solid	1	½	15 C, 5 G, 5 Gr, 10 H, 5 J	1	½	54 C, 18 G, 18 Gr, 36 H, 18 J	1	1	75 C, 25 G, 25 Gr, 50 H, 25 J
■ Bright Solids	5	¼	30 B	18	½	108 B	25	½	150 B
■ Bright Prints	9	¼	30 A, 12 K	25	¾	108 A, 31 K	33	¾	150 A, 40 K
Lining	1	3½	2 @ 30" x 59"	1	5⅞	2 @ 40" x 100"	1	8¾	3 @ 34" x 100"
Batting			59" x 59"			80" x 100"			100" x 100"

AT-A-GLANCE ROTARY CUTTING OF STRIPS AND PATCHES

Fabrics	Strip Length	Strip Width	Cross Cuts	Add'l Cuts	Yield Per Strip	Number of Strips Needed Small	Med.	Large
Ivory Solid	18"	2¾"	6 @ 2¾"	⊠	24 A	2	5	7
	18"	2¾"	6 @ 2¾"	⧄	12 H	1	3	5
	18"	2"	8 @ 2"	--	8 C	2	7	10
	18"	3"	5 @ 3"	⧄	10 D	2	8	10
	18"	2⅜"	3 @ 5⅛"	*F	6 F	1	3	5
	18"	2⅜"	3 @ 5⅛"	*Fr	6 Fr	1	3	5
	18"	2⅜"	2 @ 7¾"	*I	4 I	2	5	7
	18"	2⅜"	2 @ 7¾"	*Ir	4 Ir	2	5	7
	18"	3½"	1 @ 12", 1 @ 3½"	--	1 K, 1 M	10	36	50
	12"	3½"	1 @ 12"	--	1 M	6	12	14
Purple Print	18"	3⅞"	4 @ 3⅞"	⧄	8 E$_1$	2	5	7
	18"	5½"	3 @ 5½"	⊠	12 E$_2$	2	6	9
	18"	5⅛"	3 @ 5⅛"	⧄	6 L	2	6	9
	21¾"	21¾"	1 @ 21¾"	⊠	4 N	1	3	3
	13¼"	13¼"	1 @ 13¼"	⧄	2 O	2	2	2
Green Solid	18"	2"	8 @ 2"	--	8 C	2	7	10
	18"	1"	45°, 4 @ 2⅜"	*G	4 G	2	5	7
	18"	1"	45°, 4 @ 2⅜"	*Gr	4 Gr	2	5	7
	18"	2¾"	6 @ 2¾"	⧄	12 H	1	3	5
	18"	1"	2 @ 8¼"	--	2 J	3	9	13
Bright Solids	9"	2⅜"	3 @ 2⅜"	⧄	6 B	5	18	25
Bright Prints	9"	2¾"	3 @ 2¾"	⊠	12 A	3	9	13
	9"	3½"	2 @ 3½"	--	2 K	6	16	20

◻ For B, D, E₁, H, L, and O triangles, indicated with this icon, cut lengthwise strips and cross cuts as listed to make squares. Then cut a diagonal through each square to make pairs of triangles. (Keep the fabrics layered throughout to minimize the cutting.)

⊠ For A, E₂, and N triangles, indicated with this icon, cut strips and cross cuts as listed to make squares. Then make additional cuts across both diagonals, leaving the stacks of triangles right next to each other after the first diagonal cut.

*F For *F, cut strips 2⅜" wide and 18" long in quantities indicated. From each strip cut three pieces 5⅛" long. Trace the F patch from page 60, and cut it out on the solid cutting lines. Tape it to the underside of a rotary cutting ruler as shown. Align three edges of a stack of rectangles with the pattern. Cut the fourth edge along the edge of the ruler. Rotate the remaining half of the rectangle, align three edges, and trim the fourth along the edge of the ruler. For Fr, follow these same instructions. It is not necessary to trace and tape an Fr. Use the same F pattern as before, but turn the fabric rectangles face down when you align them for cutting Fr.

*G For *G, cut strips 1" wide and 18" long in the quantities indicated in the chart. Cut off a triangle from the lower right corner of one stack of strips at a 45° angle. Align the 2⅜" line on your rotary ruler with this cut edge of the strip. Cut along the edge of the ruler. Repeat to make four G's from a strip. For *Gr, cut off the triangle from the upper right corner instead of the lower right. Proceed to cut at 2⅜" intervals as for G.

*I For *I, cut strips 2⅜" wide and 18" long in the quantities indicated. Cut each stack of strips at 7¾" and 7¾" again to make two stacks of rectangles. Trace the I pattern and tape it to a rotary ruler as shown for F. Align three edges of a stack of rectangles with I. Cut along the edge of the ruler to complete I. Rotate the remaining half of the stack of rectangles, align three sides, and trim along the ruler for more I's. For *Ir, repeat these instructions, only when aligning the fabric rectangles with the taped I pattern, turn the fabric rectangles face down.

QUILT CONSTRUCTION

1 Pair a bright print A with a coordinating solid B. Make a second, matching pair, and set it aside for Steps 2 and 4. Complete Steps 1-4 before going on to Step 1 for the next fabric pairing. For Unit 1, sew the bright print A to an ivory solid A as shown. Press seam allowances toward the bright print.

2 Sew the second bright print A to an ivory solid A as shown to make Unit 2. Press seam allowances toward the bright print.

3 Snip off the Unit 1 and sew it to the paired bright solid B to make Unit 3 as shown. Press seams toward the bright solid B.

4 Snip off the Unit 2 and sew it to the coordinating bright solid B to make Unit 4 as shown. Press seams toward the bright solid B. Leave Units 3 and 4 connected by a twist of thread. Repeat Steps 1-4 to make the quantities indicated next to the figures at the right.

5 Complete Steps 5 and 6 for a fabric set before going on to Steps 5 and 6 for the next fabric pairing. Snip off one of the sets of Units 3 and 4. Sew an ivory C to the Unit 3 to make Unit 5 as shown. Press seams toward the C.

6 Sew the matching Unit 4 to a green solid C square to make Unit 6 as shown. Press seams toward the green square. Repeat Steps 5 and 6 to make the quantities listed for your quilt size.

7 Snip off a matching set of Units 5 and 6. Sew them together as shown to make Unit 7. Press seam allowances toward Unit 6. Repeat for all sets to make the number required for your quilt size, as listed.

8 Divide your Unit 7's into three equal piles, balancing the colors among the piles. Set aside one pile for Step 11 and one for Step 12. To each Unit 7

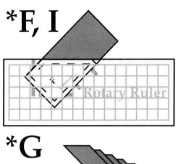

*F, I

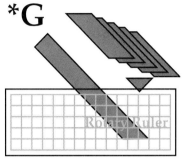

*G

Unit 1
15 (S), 54 (M), 75 (L).

Unit 2
15 (S), 54 (M), 75 (L).

Unit 3
15 (S), 54 (M), 75 (L).

Unit 4
15 (S), 54 (M), 75 (L).

Unit 5: 15 (S), 54 (M), 75 (L).

Unit 6: 15 (S), 54 (M), 75 (L).

Unit 7
Make 15 (S), 54 (M), 75 (L).

Unit 8
5 (S), 18 (M), 25 (L).

Unit 9
5 (S), 18 (M), 25 (L).

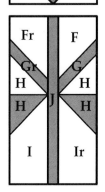

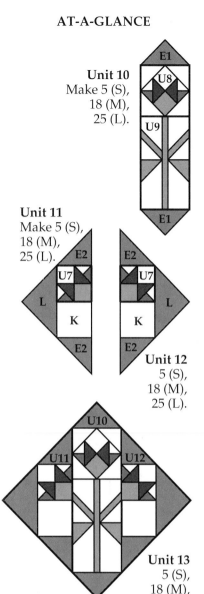

Unit 10
Make 5 (S),
18 (M),
25 (L).

Unit 11
Make 5 (S),
18 (M),
25 (L).

Unit 12
5 (S),
18 (M),
25 (L).

Unit 13
5 (S),
18 (M),
25 (L).

in the third pile, sew four ivory solid D triangles to complete Unit 8 as shown on page 59. Press seam allowances toward the D's. Make the quantity listed.

9 Referring to the diagram for Unit 9, sew an ivory Fr to a green Gr. Press seams toward the green. Add an ivory H. Again, press seams toward the green. Sew a green H to an ivory I, this time pressing seams toward the ivory. Sew this segment to the Fr-Gr-H segment as shown, pressing seams toward the green H. Similarly sew F-G-H-H-Ir for the opposite side of Unit 9. Sew the two segments together with a green J between them to complete Unit 9. Press seams toward the green J. Make the quantity listed for your quilt size.

10 Sew a Unit 8 to a Unit 9, pressing seam allowances toward Unit 9. Repeat for all Units 8 and 9. Add a purple print E_1 to the top and another to the bottom to complete Unit 10 as shown. Press seam allowances toward the E_1 triangles. Make the number listed at left for your quilt size.

11 Sew one of the Unit 7's set aside earlier to an ivory K square as shown. Press seam allowances toward the K square. Add a purple print E_2 to the top and another to the bottom. Press seams toward the purple. Add a purple L triangle to one side as shown to complete Unit 11. Press seams again toward the purple. Make the quantity indicated at left.

12 Referring to Unit 12, sew one of the remaining Unit 7's to an ivory K. Press seams toward K. Add two purple E_2's and a purple L to complete Unit 12 as shown. Press seams toward purple. Make the number listed.

13 Sew a Unit 11 and a Unit 12 to a Unit 10 as shown to complete Unit 13. Press seam allowances away from Unit 10. Use all of the Units 10, 11, and 12 to make the required number of Unit 13's as indicated.

14 Refer to the photo or drawing (pages 34 and 57) and the diagram at right as you join Unit 13's, M's, N's, O's, and bright print K's in rows. Pin at the joints before stitching.

15 Add borders, mitering or butting corners. Join the lining panels with ¼" seams. Press the quilt top and lining well. Place the lining face down. Center the batting over it, and trim excess. Place the quilt top, face up, centered over the batting. Baste through all three layers in horizontal and vertical lines about 6" apart. Quilt in the ditch between patches and along borders. Bind to finish.

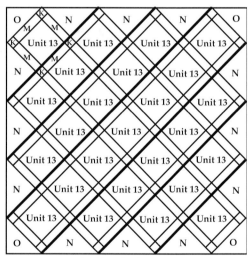

Large Quilt Piecing Diagram

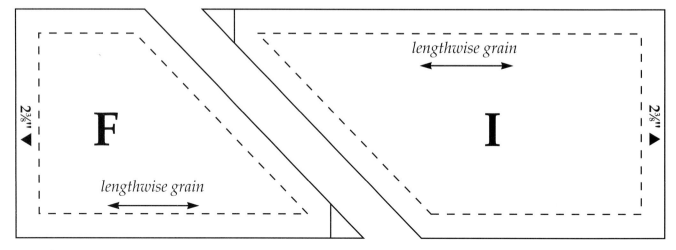

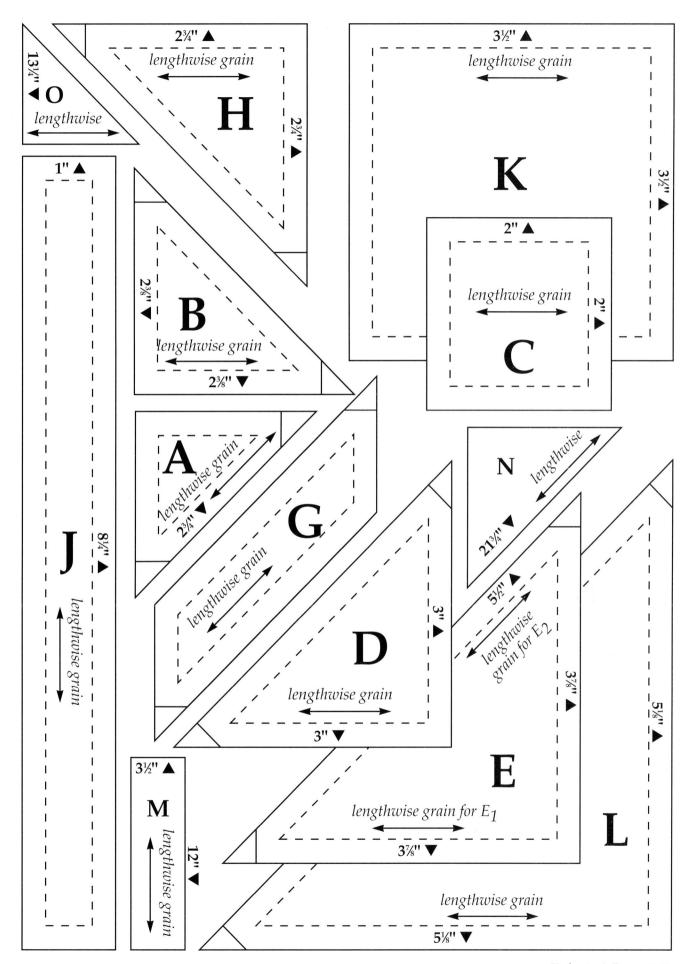

13¼" ◄ O
lengthwise

2¾" ▲ H
lengthwise grain
2¾" ▶

3½" ▲ K
lengthwise grain
3½" ▶

1" ▲ J
2⅜" ◄ B
lengthwise grain
2⅜" ▼

2" ▲ C
lengthwise grain
2" ▶

A
lengthwise grain
2¾" ▶

G
lengthwise grain

8¼" ▶

J
lengthwise grain

N
lengthwise
21¾" ▶

5½" D
lengthwise grain for E₂
3" ▶
lengthwise grain
3" ▼

3⅞" ▶

5⅛" ▶

E
lengthwise grain for E₁
3⅞" ▼

L

3½" ▲ M
lengthwise grain
12" ▼

lengthwise grain
5⅛" ▼

PICKET FENCE

Picket Fence is one of those cleverly simple designs that looks as though it has been a favorite pattern for generations, although it is brand new. Perhaps it is the familiarity of the sawtooth and fence rails elements or of the red and white Robbing-Peter-to-Pay-Paul coloring that gives this pattern its ageless appeal. The full-page color photograph is on page 35. Directions follow for the quilt in three sizes: 53½" square for a wall quilt or throw (below); 62" x 79" for the twin quilt in the photograph; and 104½" square for a queen or king size.

WHAT MAKES THIS QUILT EASY?

✔ The Picket Fence has super-simple blocks of just eight pieces.

✔ The body of the quilt has just two basic pattern pieces. Make a block in three quick steps.

✔ Handsome, wide borders and a diagonal set reduce the number of blocks needed.

✔ Classic two-color design makes fabric selection a matter of simple contrasts.

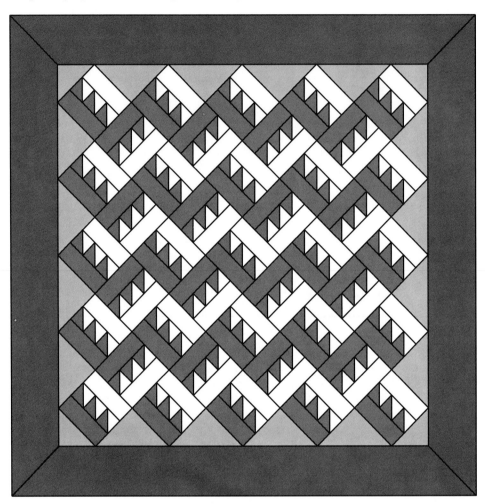

My Picket Fence quilt was made in a favorite old color scheme of red and white. Reds range from orange to wine and everything in between. Whites tend to the creamy side, with some pale peach and tan thrown in. Edge triangles are a shade lighter than the reds, with salmon, coral and peachy pink prints.

OTHER STUNNING COLORS

◆ Blue and White. Another classic two-color scheme features medium blues, bright blues, and navy blues against crisp whites, off-whites, and beiges. Edge triangles in baby blue to periwinkle complete the quilt.

◆ Multicolored bright prints contrasting with white and bright yellow.

◆ Deep fall shades contrasting with tawny, warm lights.

PICKET FENCE YARDAGE AND CUTTING REQUIREMENTS

Fabrics	Small - 53½" x 53½" No. Pcs.	Tot. Yds.	Patches	Medium - 62" x 79" No. Pcs.	Tot. Yds.	Patches	Large - 104½" x 104½" No. Pcs.	Tot. Yds.	Patches
☐ Cream Prints	11	1½	123 A, 41 B	21	2¼	249 A, 83 B	56	4¾	663 A, 221 B
■ Red Prints	11	1½	123 A, 41 B	21	2¼	249 A, 83 B	56	4¾	663 A, 221 B
▨ Coral Prints	6	⅜	16 C, 4 D	8	⅝	24 C, 4 D	12	1	40 C, 4 D
Border	1	1¾	4 @ 6" x 54"	1	2⅜	2 @ 6" x 62½" 2 @ 6" x 79½"	1	3⅛	4 @ 6" x 105"
(binding)	1	(1¾)	4 @ 1½" x 56"	1	(2⅜)	2 @ 1½" x 64" 2 @ 1½" x 81"	1	(3⅛)	4 @ 1½" x 107"
Lining	1	3⅜	2 @ 29" x 57"	1	3⅞	2 @ 42" x 66"	1	9⅝	3 @ 37" x 109"
Batting			57" x 57"			66" x 83"			108" x 108"

AT-A-GLANCE ROTARY CUTTING OF STRIPS AND PATCHES

Fabrics	Strip Length	Strip Width	Cross Cuts	Add'l Cuts	Yield Per Strip	Number of Strips Needed Small	Med.	Large
Cream Prints	18"	2⅞"	6 @ 2⅞"	◺	12 A	11	21	56
	13½"	2½"	2 @ 6½"	--	2 B	21	42	111
Red Prints	18"	2⅞"	6 @ 2⅞"	◺	12 A	11	21	56
	13½"	2½"	2 @ 6½"	--	2 B	21	42	111
Coral Prints	9¾"	9¾"	1 @ 9¾"	⊠	4 C	4	6	10
	5⅛"	5⅛"	1 @ 5⅛"	◺	2D	2	2	2

SPECIAL ROTARY CUTTING INSTRUCTIONS

◺ For the A and D triangles, indicated with this icon, cut lengthwise strips and cross cuts as listed to make squares. Then cut a diagonal through each square to complete A and D triangles. (Keep the fabrics layered throughout to minimize the cutting.)

⊠ For the C triangles, indicated with this icon, cut strips and cross cuts as listed to make squares. Then make additional cuts across both diagonals, leaving the stacks of triangles right next to each other after the first diagonal cut.

QUILT CONSTRUCTION

1 Sew a red print A triangle to a cream print A along their long edges. Press seam allowances open. That is, press the red toward the red and the cream toward the cream. This completes a Unit 1. Repeat for all A's to make the quantity listed for your quilt size.

2 Sew three Unit 1's in a row as shown to complete Unit 2. Press seam allowances toward the red triangles. Make the quantity listed at right. Note that you will have many Unit 1's left over at this stage. They will be used to make Unit 3's.

3 Turn the remaining Unit 1's 90° so that the red is at the bottom and right. Sew three Unit 1's in a row as shown to complete Unit 3. Press seam allowances toward the red triangles. Repeat for all remaining Unit 1's to make the listed number of Unit 3's.

4 Sew a cream B rectangle to the cream edge of a Unit 2. Sew a red B rectangle to the red edge of the same Unit 2 to complete Unit 4 as shown at right. Press seam allowances away from the Unit 2. Repeat for all of the Unit 2's to make the quantity listed.

AT-A-GLANCE

Unit 1
Make 123 (S), 249 (M), 663 (L).

Unit 2
Make 25 (S), 48 (M), 121 (L).

Unit 3
Make 16 (S), 35 (M), 100 (L).

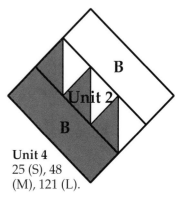

Unit 4
25 (S), 48 (M), 121 (L).

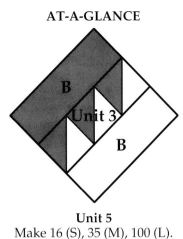

Unit 5
Make 16 (S), 35 (M), 100 (L).

5 Sew a cream B rectangle to the cream edge of a Unit 3. Sew a red B rectangle to the red edge of the same Unit 3 to complete Unit 5 as shown. Press seam allowances away from the Unit 3. Repeat for all Unit 3's to make the quantity listed for your chosen size. You should have no B rectangles or Unit 3's left over.

6 Stack all of the Unit 4's with the cream rectangle at the top right, and stack all of the Unit 5's with the cream rectangle at the bottom right as shown. Lay out the quilt on the floor. See the photo or drawing for your quilt size. The rows run diagonally across the quilt, and you will sew the units into rows of varying lengths. The first row, starting in the upper left corner, is made up of a D triangle, a C triangle, a Unit 4, and another C triangle. The second row will have C-Unit 4-Unit 5-Unit 4-C. The third row will have C-Unit 4-Unit 5-Unit 4-Unit 5-Unit 4-C. Continue laying out the quilt, following the picture. Once you have laid out all of the units and edge triangles, stand back and look to make sure everything is turned properly. Adjust unit placement to achieve a good balance of color. In the top left corner of the leftmost unit in each row, pin a paper label marked with the row number. Pick up and stack the blocks and triangles in sequence, keeping them turned as they were in your layout. Place the last triangle on the bottom of the stack, then the next-to-last triangle, and so on, with the first row patches and units on the top of the stack. Join the triangles and units into rows. Pin at the corners of each unit, opposing seams. Press seams toward the Unit 4's. Join the rows to complete the quilt top, again opposing seams and pinning joints. Press seam allowances toward the bottom of the quilt.

7 Add borders, butting or mitering corners as you desire. Seam the lining panels. Press the quilt top and lining. Mark the quilting design of your choice in the edge triangles and borders. Lay the lining face down and center the batting over it. Position the quilt top, face up, over the batting. Baste the layers together every four inches or so. Quilt in the ditch between all patches. Quilt the edge triangles and borders as marked. Bind to finish.

**Diagram of
Large Picket Fence,
Showing Diagonal Rows.**

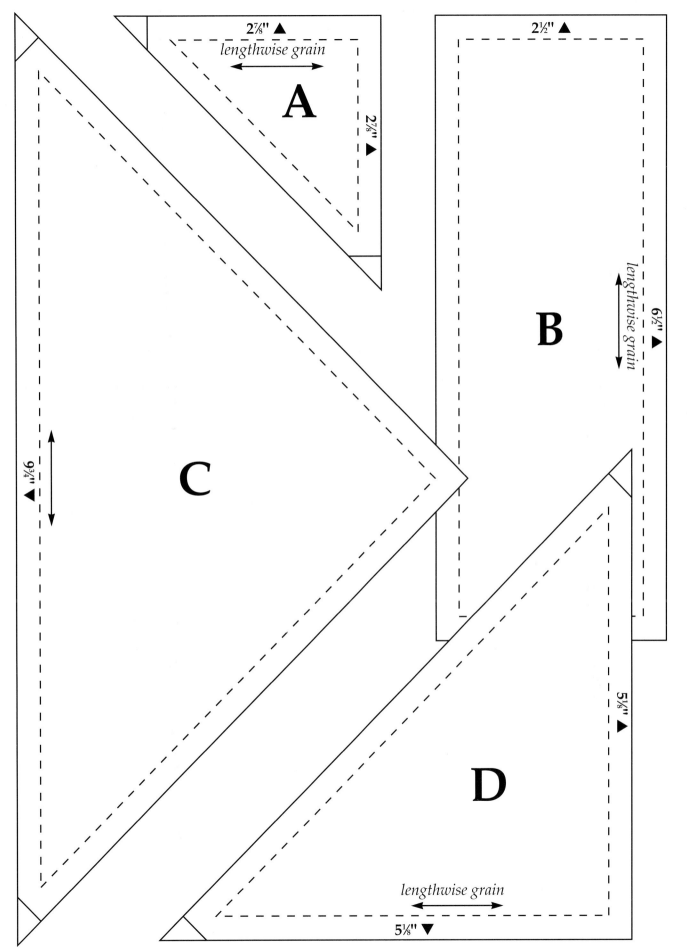

2⅞" ▲

lengthwise grain

A

2⅞" ▶

2½" ▲

B

6½" ▶

lengthwise grain

9¾" ▲

C

5⅛" ▶

D

lengthwise grain

5⅛" ▼

ROAD TO COLORADO

The Road to Colorado is a new Nine-Patch variation with a handsome built-in border. With modern rotary methods, this quilt is easier to make than its traditonal counterparts, yet it looks more intricate with its extra-special touches. The quilt photo is on page 36. The quilt is presented in two sizes, a 49¼" square wall quilt (below) and a 71⅞" x 94½" twin or double coverlet (photographed).

WHAT MAKES THIS QUILT EASY?

✔ The body of the quilt is simply squares and rectangles. They are easy to cut and sew, and perfect joints are easily achieved.

✔ The rhombus-shaped edge patches eliminate the need to fuss with points around the perimeter of the quilt.

✔ The straight grain on the rhombus patches is along the outside of the quilt, a trick that lets you handle the quilt top without stretchy bias edges.

✔ Extra-easy blocks have just nine pieces, all squares. Stitch a block in minutes!

I made Road to Colorado as a Scrap Quilt with an assortment of cream, light tan, and white prints in the background. These creamy colors are combined with turquoise and teal prints for half of the Nine-Patch blocks and with pink to rose prints plus light and dark brown for the remaining nine-patch blocks.

OTHER STUNNING COLORS

◆ Red, parchment, navy, and golden tan. For a country look, substitute navy for teal in the chains and red for pink. Make the cream background and brown accents a little more golden for a warm, cozy glow.

◆ Ivory background, pumpkin accents, and turkey red with forest green chains.

◆ White background, baby blue accents, and medium blue with navy chains.

◆ Off-white background, gold accents, and green with black chains.

ROAD TO COLORADO YARDAGE AND CUTTING REQUIREMENTS

Fabrics	Small - 49¼" x 49¼"			Medium - 71⅞" x 94½"		
	No. Pcs.	Tot. Yds.	Patches	No. Pcs.	Tot. Yds.	Patches
☐ Cream Prints	12	1⅞	64 A, 36 B, 28 C, 28 Cr, 8 D, 4 E, 4 F	38	4⅛	260 A, 140 B, 52 C, 52 Cr, 20 D, 4 E, 4 F
■ Brown Prints	9	½	60 A	19	1	128 A
■ Pink Prints	10	½	68 A	28	1	196 A
■ Teal Prints	15	½	105 A	24	1½	329 A
Border	1	1½	4 @ 2½" x 49¾"	1	2⅞	2 @ 2½" x 95" 2 @ 2½" x 72⅜"
(binding)		(1½)	4 @ 1½" x 51"		(2⅞)	2 @ 1½" x 96½" 2 @ 1½" x 74"
Lining	1	3⅛	2 @ 27" x 53"	1	5¾	2 @ 38½" x 98½"
Batting			53" x 53"			76" x 98½"

AT-A-GLANCE ROTARY CUTTING OF STRIPS AND PATCHES

Fabrics	Strip Length	Strip Width	Cross Cuts	Add'l Cuts	Yield Per Strip	Number of Strips Needed	
						Small	Medium
Cream Prints	18"	2½"	7 @ 2½"	--	7 A	10	38
	13½"	2½"	2 @ 6½"	--	2 B	18	70
	18"	5¼"	45°, 3 @ 2½"	*C	6 C	5	9
	18"	5¼"	45°, 3 @ 2½"	*Cr	6 Cr	5	9
	14"	2½"	3 @ 4½"	--	3 D	3	7
	2⅞"	2⅞"	1 @ 2⅞"	◻	2 E	2	2
	*F	*F	--	*F	--	--	--
Brown Prints	18"	2½"	7 @ 2½"	--	7 A	9	19
Pink Prints	18"	2½"	7 @ 2½"	--	7 A	10	28
Teal Prints	18"	2½"	7 @ 2½"	--	7 A	15	47

SPECIAL ROTARY CUTTING INSTRUCTIONS

AT-A-GLANCE

◻ After cutting lengthwise strips and cross cuts as listed to make squares, make additional cuts for E triangles, indicated with this icon, by cutting a diagonal through each square. (Keep the fabrics layered throughout to minimize the cutting.)

*C For C, cut strips 5¼" wide and 18" long in the quantities indicated. Cut off the lower right corner of a strip at a 45° angle. Align the 2½" line on your ruler with this cut edge of the strip. Cut three pieces at 2½" intervals. Trace and tape a C pattern to the underside of your rotary ruler as shown. Align a stack of fabric pieces with three edges of the pattern and cut along the edge of the ruler to make a stack of C's. Rotate the remainder to align it with the pattern, and trim along the ruler for another stack of C's. For Cr, cut strips 5¼" wide and 18" long. Cut off the upper right corner at a 45° angle. Cut three pieces at 2½" intervals. Turn these pieces face down to align with the C pattern and cut along edge of ruler.

*F For F, start with two leftover Cr's, face up. Stack these neatly with two C's, face down. You can tape the F pattern to you ruler if you like, but since you already traced the C pattern for the previous step, you may find it easier to use that. Tape the C to the underside of your rotary ruler as shown. (This is in a different position than it was in when you taped it to the ruler for C.) Align the square end of the stack of C's and Cr's with the C pattern. Cut off the point of the C's and Cr's along the edge of the ruler to complete four F's.

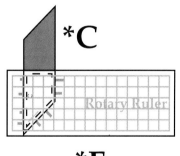

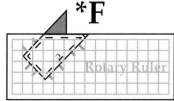

AT-A-GLANCE

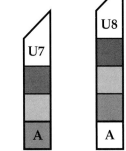

Unit 1
8 (S),
48 (M).

| A | A | A |

Unit 2
4 (S),
24 (M).

| A | A | A |

Unit 3
Make
4 (S),
24 (M).

	U 1	
	U 2	
	U 1	

Unit 4
18 (S),
70 (M).

| A | A | A |

Unit 5
9 (S),
35 (M).

| A | A | A |

Unit 6
9 (S),
35 (M).

	U 4	
	U 5	
	U 4	

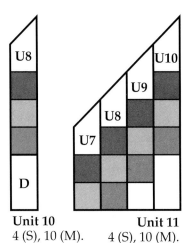

Unit 7
24 (S),
48 (M).

Unit 8
16 (S),
34 (M).

Unit 9
4 (S),
10 (M).

Unit 10
4 (S), 10 (M).

Unit 11
4 (S), 10 (M).

QUILT CONSTRUCTION

1 Note that you will have leftover patches throughout most of the unit construction. Make only the number listed for your quilt size; don't continue until all of the cream squares are sewn to all of the pink squares, for example. Use a variety of prints for each color in a unit. Sew two cream print A squares to a pink print A to make Unit 1 as shown. Press seam allowances toward the pink square.

2 Sew two pink print A squares to a brown print A to make Unit 2 as shown. Press seam allowances toward the pink squares. Make the quantity indicated.

3 Sew two Unit 1's to a Unit 2 as shown to complete Unit 3. Press seam allowances toward the Unit 2. Make the number listed.

4 Sew two teal print A squares to a cream print A to complete Unit 4 as shown. Press seam allowances toward the teal squares. Make the quantity indicated for your quilt size.

5 Sew two cream print A squares to a teal print A as shown to make Unit 5. Press seam allowances toward the teal square. Make the number required for your quilt size.

6 Sew two Unit 4's to a Unit 5 to complete Unit 6 as shown. Press seam allowances toward the Unit 4's. Make the number listed at left.

7 Sew a cream print C to a brown print A square to a pink print A. Press seam allowances toward the brown square. Make the number shown.

8 Add a teal print A square to some Unit 7's to complete Unit 8 as shown. Press seam allowances toward the teal square. Make the listed quantity.

9 Add a cream print A square to some Unit 8's to make Unit 9 as shown. Press seams toward Unit 8. Make the number indicated.

10 Add a cream print D rectangle to some Unit 8's to make Unit 10 as shown. Press seams toward Unit 8. Make the number listed.

11 See the diagram for Unit 11. Sew a Unit 7 to a Unit 8 to a Unit 9 to a Unit 10 to make Unit 11 as shown. Oppose seams at the corners of the squares and pin at these joints before stitching. Press seam allowances toward Unit 10. Make the number listed.

12 Units 12-16 echo Units 7-11, only reversed. Sew a cream print Cr to a brown print A square to a pink print A to complete Unit 12 as shown. Press seams toward the brown. Make the quantity indicated for your quilt size.

13 Add a teal print A square to some Unit 12's to make Unit 13 as shown. Press this new seam allowance toward the teal square. Make the number listed for your quilt size.

14 Add a cream print A square to some Unit 13's to make Unit 14 as shown. Press this new seam allowance toward Unit 13. Make the quantity listed for the quilt in your chosen size.

15 Add a cream print D rectangle to some Unit 13's to make Unit 15 as shown. Press seams toward Unit 13. Make the quantity listed.

16 Sew a Unit 12 to a Unit 13 to a Unit 14 to a Unit 15 as shown to make Unit 16. Oppose seams at the corners of the squares and pin at these joints. Press seam allowances toward Unit 15. Make the number listed.

17 Sew a Cream print F to a brown print A to a pink print A to a teal print A to a cream print A to make Unit 17 as shown. Press seam allowances toward the brown square and the teal square. Make four of these units, whether you are making the small or medium size quilt.

18 Join Units 7, 8, 17, 13, and 12 as shown to make Unit 18. Oppose seams and pin at the joints. Press seam allowances toward Unit 17. Make four of these units.

19 Refer to the Unit 19 figure. Sew a cream print Cr to a brown print A square. Press seams toward the brown square. Sew a cream print E to a cream print C as shown. Press the seam allowances toward the E triangle. Join the Cr-A segment to the E-C segment, opposing seams and pinning at the joint in the middle. Press seams toward the brown. This completes Unit 19. Make four Unit 19's.

20 Refer to the Unit 20 figure. Sew two cream print B rectangles to opposite sides of a Unit 6. Press seams toward the rectangles. Sew two teal print squares to opposite ends of a third cream print B rectangle. Press seam allowances toward the B rectangle. Add this to the B-Unit 6-B segment, opposing seams and pinning at the joints. Press seam allowances away from Unit 6. This completes Unit 20. Make four Unit 20's.

21 **For the medium size quilt,** refer to the figure below. First make the unshaded segment: Join teal A squares and cream B rectangles to make rows across the unshaded square segment. Join cream B's plus Units 3 and 6 as shown to make rows. Join rows to complete the square segment. Next join the units and patches into rows as shown for the lightly shaded segments. Sew these to the unshaded segment. Finally, make the darker shaded units, sewing units and patches into rows as indicated by the heavy lines. Sew these two darker shaded segments to the segments already joined to complete the quilt top. Add teal borders, mitering corners or butting them, as desired.

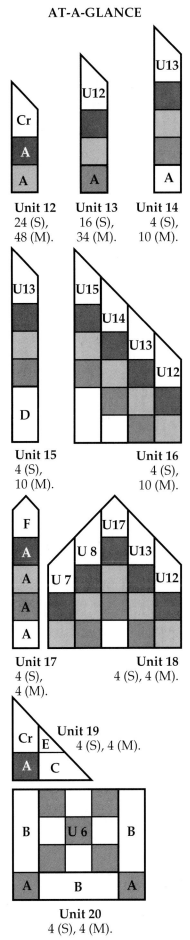

AT-A-GLANCE

Unit 12
24 (S),
48 (M).

Unit 13
16 (S),
34 (M).

Unit 14
4 (S),
10 (M).

Unit 15
4 (S),
10 (M).

Unit 16
4 (S),
10 (M).

Unit 17
4 (S),
4 (M).

Unit 18
4 (S), 4 (M).

Unit 19
4 (S), 4 (M).

Unit 20
4 (S), 4 (M).

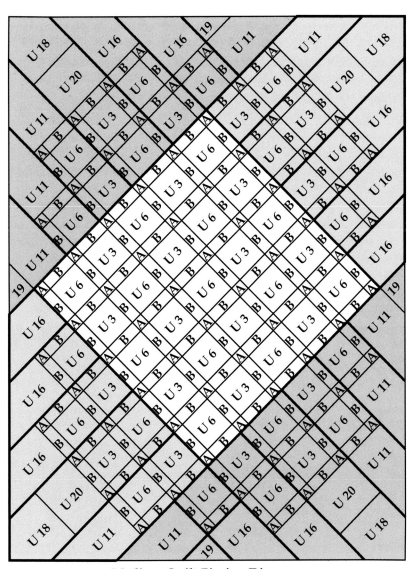

Medium Quilt Piecing Diagram

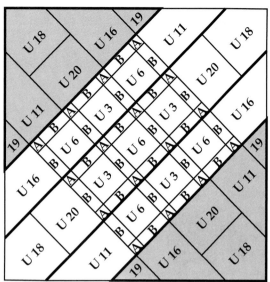

For the small size quilt, refer to the figure at left. Start with the unshaded section. Join teal A squares and cream B rectangles to make sash rows across the middle of the unshaded area. Join cream B's plus Units 3 and 6 as shown to make block rows, as well. Join a sash row to a block row. Add a Unit 11 at one end and a Unit 16 at the other end as shown to make a row across the quilt. Repeat. Join two sash rows to a block row. Add a Unit 20 and a Unit 18 to each end. Join the three rows to complete the unshaded segment. Then make the shaded sections, first joining Units 18 and 20, then joining them with the other units as shown. Join the three sections. Add teal borders, mitering or butting corners, as desired.

22 **For both sizes,** join the lining panels. Press top and lining well. Place the lining face down. Center the batting over it, and trim excess. Place the quilt top, face up, centered over the batting. Baste through all three layers in horizontal and vertical lines about 6" apart. Quilt in the ditch between patches and along border seams. Bind to finish.

Small Quilt Piecing Diagram

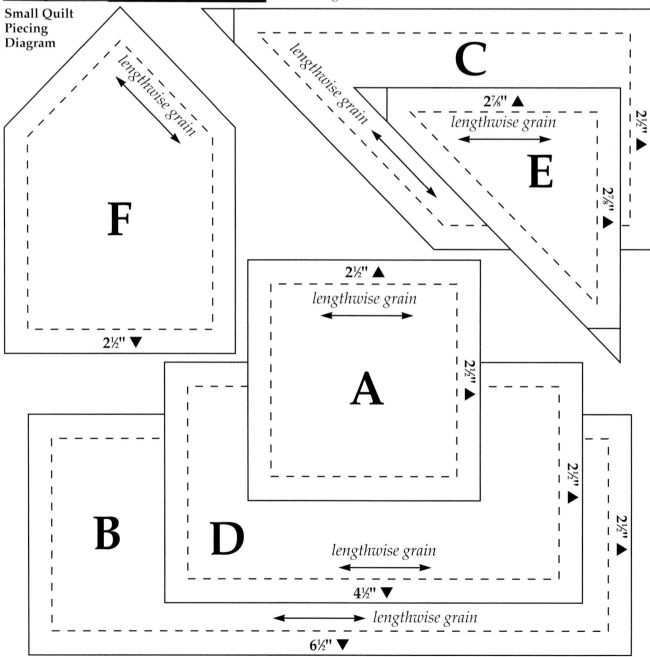

VIRGINIA PINWHEEL

Virginia Pinwheel combines favorite traditional patterns, the Pinwheel and Virginia Reel, in a design with splendid visual movement and subtle scrap effects. The color photo is on page 37. Directions for this quilt are in three sizes, a 56" x 56" wall quilt shown below, an 80" x 104" twin spread or double coverlet (photographed), and a 104" square queen spread or king coverlet.

I made this quilt with an assortment of brown, blue, and cream prints for the reels and black, navy, and tan prints for the pinwheel elements. The pinwheel colors were selected to be a shade darker than the neighboring patches.

OTHER STUNNING COLORS

◆ Multicolored bright prints and light prints for the reels; 1930's green and yellow solids for the pinwheels. This is an entirely different look from the photographed version. Busy, colorful prints with a depression-era look are what I envision here. Substitute a mixed bag of bright prints--red, blue, green, pink, purple, and orange--for both the brown and the blue. Prints in various bright colors on white backgrounds substitute for the cream. Green pinwheels accent the light reels and butter yellow pinwheels accent the bright reels.

◆ Scarlet, medium blue, and off-white with turkey red, navy, and tan pinwheels.

◆ Peach, brown, and cream with rust, black, and tan pinwheels.

◆ Rose, medium blue and white with wine, navy, and silver pinwheels.

◆ Medium blue, medium purple, and white with navy, dark purple, and light blue and lavender pinwheels.

WHAT MAKES THIS QUILT EASY?

✔ This quilt has just 24 patches in a big 12" block. That's about half the number in a typical block.

✔ Just four pattern pieces, simple squares and triangles.

✔ The patches were designed for rotary cutting, with easy-to-measure dimensions. (This block in any other size would pose problems in either rotary cutting or piecing.)

✔ Fabric grain was carefully considered in planning this quilt. Each unit has straight grain all around the edges to make handing easy throughout the construction process.

VIRGINIA PINWHEEL YARDAGE AND CUTTING REQUIREMENTS

Fabrics	Small - 56" x 56"			Medium - 80" x 104"			Large - 104" x104"		
	No. Pcs.	Tot. Yds.	Patches	No. Pcs.	Tot. Yds.	Patches	No. Pcs.	Tot. Yds.	Patches
Brown Prints	16	¾	16 A, 16 B, 16 C, 16 D_1, 16 D_2	24	2	48 A, 48 B, 48 C, 48 D_1, 48 D_2	32	2¾	64 A, 64 B, 64 C, 64 D_1, 64 D_2
Blue Prints	16	¾	16 A, 16 B, 16 C, 16 D_1, 16 D_2	24	2	48 A, 48 B, 48 C, 48 D_1, 48 D_2	32	2¾	64 A, 64 B, 64 C, 64 D_1, 64 D_2
Cream Prints	16	1½	32 A, 32 B, 32 C, 32 D_1, 32 D_2	24	3½	96 A, 96 B, 96 C, 96 D_1, 96 D_2	32	4½	128 A, 128 B, 128 C, 128 D_1, 128 D_2
Black Prints	4	¼	16 D_2	12	¾	48 D_2	16	¾	64 D_2
Navy Prints	4	¼	16 D_2	12	¾	48 D_2	16	¾	64 D_2
Beige Prints	4	½	32 D_2	12	1½	96 D_2	16	1½	128 D_2
Brown Border	1	1½	4 @ 1" x 49½"	1	2⅞	2 @ 1" x 73½" 2 @ 1" x 97½"	1	2⅞	4 @ 1" x 97½"
Blue Border	1	1¾	4 @ 4" x 56½"	1	3⅛	2 @ 4" x 80½" 2 @ 4" x 104½"	1	3⅛	4 @ 4" x 104½"
(binding)		(1¾)	4 @ 1½" x 58"		(3⅛)	2 @ 1½" x 106" 2 @ 1½" x 82"		(3⅛)	4 @ 1½" x 106"
Lining Batting	1	3½	2 @ 30½" x 60" 60" x 60"	1	6⅜	2 @ 42½" x 108" 84" x 108"	1	9½	3 @ 36½" x 108" 108" x 108"

AT-A-GLANCE ROTARY CUTTING OF STRIPS AND PATCHES

Fabrics	Strip Length	Strip Width	Cross Cuts	Add'l Cuts	Yield Per Strip	Number of Strips Needed		
						Small	Med.	Large
Brown Prints	9"	2"	4 @ 2"	--	4 A	4	12	16
	9"	3"	2 @ 3"	◻	4 B	4	12	16
	9"	3⅞"	2 @ 3⅞"	◻	4 C	4	12	16
	9"	5⅛"	1 @ 5⅛"	◻	2 D_1	8	24	32
	9"	7¼"	1 @ 7¼"	⊠	4 D_2	4	12	16
Blue Prints	9"	2"	4 @ 2"	--	4 A	4	12	16
	9"	3"	2 @ 3"	◻	4 B	4	12	16
	9"	3⅞"	2 @ 3⅞"	◻	4 C	4	12	16
	9"	5⅛"	1 @ 5⅛"	◻	2 D_1	8	24	32
	9"	7¼"	1 @ 7¼"	⊠	4 D_2	4	12	16
Cream Prints	18"	2"	8 @ 2"	--	8 A	4	12	16
	18"	3"	5 @ 3"	◻	10 B	4	10	13
	18"	3⅞"	4 @ 3⅞"	◻	8 C	4	12	16
	18"	5⅛"	3 @ 5⅛"	◻	6 D_1	6	16	22
	18"	7¼"	2 @ 7¼"	⊠	8 D_2	4	12	16
Black Prints	9"	7¼"	1 @ 7¼"	⊠	4 D_2	4	12	16
Navy Prints	9"	7¼"	1 @ 7¼"	⊠	4 D_2	4	12	16
Beige Prints	18"	7¼"	2 @ 7¼"	⊠	8 D_2	4	12	16

SPECIAL ROTARY CUTTING INSTRUCTIONS

◻ For B, C, and D_1 triangles, cut lengthwise strips and cross cuts as listed to make squares. Then make additional cuts for these triangles, indicated with this icon, by cutting a diagonal through each square. (Keep the fabrics layered throughout to minimize the cutting.)

⊠ For the D_2 triangles, indicated with this icon, cut strips and make cross cuts as listed to make squares. Then make additional cuts across both diagonals, leaving the stacks of triangles right next to each other after the first diagonal cut. This will help you make the second diagonal cut pefectly.

QUILT CONSTRUCTION

1 Set aside half of the cream A squares cut from each fabric. You will need these for Step 2. To one of the remaining cream A squares, sew a brown A square. Press seam allowances toward the brown square. This completes Unit 1. Repeat for each brown square to make the number of units listed at top right.

2 To one of the cream A squares set aside earlier, sew a blue A square. Press the seam allowance toward the blue square. This completes Unit 2. Repeat for each blue square to make the number of units listed at right.

3 Join a Unit 1 to a Unit 2 as shown, with blue squares and brown squares touching cream squares. Press seam allowances toward the Unit 1. This completes Unit 3. Repeat for each Unit 1 and Unit 2 to make the number listed.

4 Turn a Unit 3 so that the brown square is in the upper left corner. (This will be considered right-side-up throughout this step.) Sew a brown B triangle to the top of the unit. Press the triangle away from the center of the unit. Now, add a cream B triangle to the right side of the unit. Press the cream triangle away from the unit center. Sew a blue B triangle to the bottom of the unit. Press the blue triangle away from the unit center. Sew a cream B triangle to the left side of the unit. Press the cream triangle away from the center of the unit. This completes Unit 4. Repeat for each Unit 3 to make the number of units listed.

5 Turn a Unit 4 so that the brown B triangle is at the top. (This will be considered right-side-up throughout this step.) Sew a brown C triangle to the top right corner of the unit. Press the triangle away from the center of the unit. Now, add a cream C triangle to the bottom right corner of the unit. Press the cream triangle away from the unit center. Sew a blue C triangle to the bottom left corner of the unit. Press the blue triangle away from the unit center. Sew a cream C triangle to the upper left corner of the unit. Press the cream triangle away from the center of the unit. This completes Unit 5. Repeat for each Unit 4 to make the number of units listed at right.

6 Set aside for Steps 7-9 the blue, brown, and cream D_2 triangles, which have the straight grain along the long edge. Turn a Unit 5 so that the brown C triangle is in the upper right corner. (This will be considered right-side-up throughout this step.) Add D_1 triangles (the ones cut with the short sides on the straight grain) as follows: Sew a brown D_1 to the right side of the unit. Press the triangle away from the center of the unit. Now, add a cream D_1 to the bottom. Press the cream triangle away from the center. Sew a blue D_1 to the left side. Press the blue triangle away from the unit center. Sew a cream D_1 to the top of the unit. Press the cream triangle away from the center of the unit. This completes Unit 6. Repeat for each Unit 5 to make the number of units listed.

7 To one of the blue D_2 triangles set aside earlier, sew a navy D_2 triangle, as shown. Press seam allowances toward the navy. This completes Unit 7. Repeat for each of the remaining navy and blue D_2 triangles to make the number of units listed at right. Navy triangles must be on the left, as shown.

8 To one of the brown D_2 triangles set aside earlier, sew a black D_2 triangle, as shown. Press seam allowances toward the black. This completes Unit 8. Repeat for all remaining black and brown D_2 triangles to make the number of units listed at right. Black triangles must be on the right, as shown.

9 To one of the cream D_2 triangles set aside earlier, sew a beige D_2 triangle as shown. Press seam allowances toward the beige. This completes Unit 9. Repeat for all cream and beige D_2 triangles to make the number of units listed at right. Cream triangles must be on the left, as shown, in every Unit 9.

10 Turn a Unit 6 so that the brown D_1 triangle is at the right. (This will be right-side-up throughout this step.) Sew a Unit 7 to the upper left corner of the Unit 6. Press the Unit 7 away from the center of the block. Sew a Unit 8 to the lower right corner, and press Unit 8 away from the center. Sew one Unit 9 to

AT-A-GLANCE

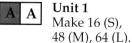
Unit 1
Make 16 (S), 48 (M), 64 (L).

Unit 2
Make 16 (S), 48 (M), 64 (L).

Unit 3
Make 16 (S), 48 (M), 64 (L).

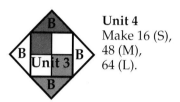
Unit 4
Make 16 (S), 48 (M), 64 (L).

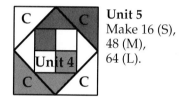
Unit 5
Make 16 (S), 48 (M), 64 (L).

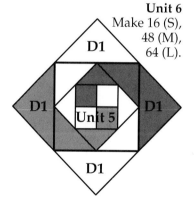
Unit 6
Make 16 (S), 48 (M), 64 (L).

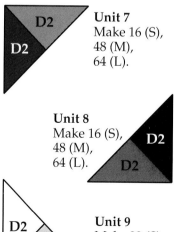
Unit 7
Make 16 (S), 48 (M), 64 (L).

Unit 8
Make 16 (S), 48 (M), 64 (L).

Unit 9
Make 32 (S), 96 (M), 128 (L).

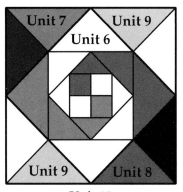

Unit 10
Make 16 (S), 48 (M), 64 (L).

the upper right corner and another Unit 9 to the lower left corner, and press both away from the center. This completes Unit 10 (the quilt block). Repeat for each Unit 6 to make the number of blocks indicated at left.

11 Referring to the quilt photograph on page 37 or the drawing on page 71, arrange blocks in 4 rows of 4 (small), 8 rows of 6 (medium), or 8 rows of 8 blocks each (large). Turn blocks so that brown D_2 triangles always touch black triangles and blue D_2 triangles touch navy triangles in the block corners. Join the blocks into rows, opposing seams as pressed and pinning at the block corners. Press seam allowances between blocks to the right in one row and to the left in the next row. Join the rows, again pinning at the joints and opposing seams. Press the row seams toward the bottom of the quilt.

12 Sew brown border strips to blue border strips, using ¼" seam allowances, and matching centers. **For the medium size quilt,** be sure to pair the long brown strips with the long blue strips and the short brown strips with the short blue strips. The longer strips are for the sides of the quilt. The shorter strips are for the top and bottom. **For all sizes,** Sew one pair of border strips to the side of the quilt, again matching centers. Repeat for the other three sides. Miter the corners to complete the quilt top.

13 Join the lining panels with one or more lengthwise seams of ¼". Press top and lining well. Place the lining face down. Center the batting over it, and trim away the excess. Place the quilt top, face up, centered over the batting. Baste through all three layers, starting at the center and working your way toward the edges in horizontal and vertical lines about 6" apart. Quilt in the ditch between patches and along border seams. Bind to finish.

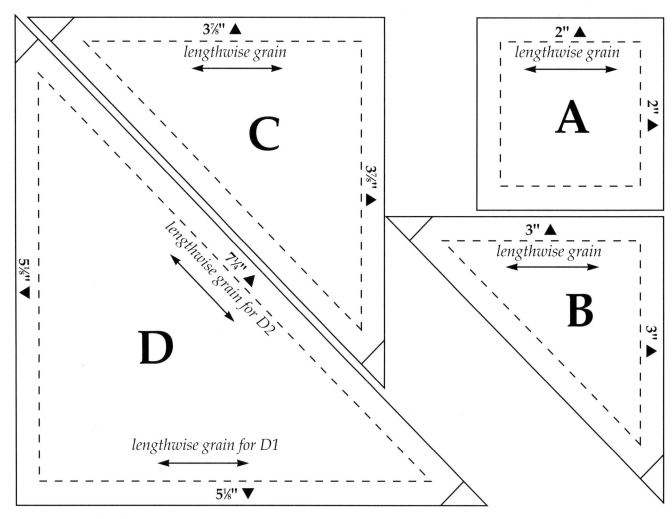

WILLIAM'S STAR & CROSS

William's Star & Cross comes together so quickly and easily that you will want to make it over and over again in a variety of color schemes. Try it in the colors I used (photo on page 38) or in the other attractive color schemes suggested below and on pages 47-48. The quilt is presented as a 41¾" x 56⅝" baby quilt, a 71½" x 86¼" twin or double coverlet, or an 86¼" x 86¼" double or queen size quilt.

WHAT MAKES THIS QUILT EASY?

✔ Thanks to its unique design, the can't-miss points in William's Star and Cross will be crisp and precisely pointed even if your sewing is less than perfect.

✔ The large and small triangles forming these star points make matching easy and they make the joints less bulky than those in other stars.

✔ The extra-easy blocks have just nine pieces, simple squares and rectangles.

✔ This quilt can be made with very little pinning and joint matching. The pieced sashes require no pinning at all; the blocks require only two pins in each of two seams; block and sash rows can be made without pins.

I made this quilt in an assortment of scrap prints in reds, whites, blacks, and a few golds for accent. I allowed the reds to range from red-orange to cinnamon to wine because I wanted to make sure that the individual patches were well defined while contributing to the starry effect.

OTHER STUNNING COLORS

◆ Brown, cream, teal, and gold. I'd make star patches from golden tan to chocolate and black. Creamy backgrounds could go from white to light gold. Teal would substitute for the black in the crosses, with gold once again as an accent.

WILLIAM'S STAR & CROSS YARDAGE AND CUTTING REQUIREMENTS

Fabrics	Small - 41¾" x 56⅝" No. Pcs.	Tot. Yds.	Patches	Medium - 71½" x 86¼" No. Pcs.	Tot. Yds.	Patches	Large - 86¼" x 86¼" No. Pcs.	Tot. Yds.	Patches
Red Prints	12	¾	8 C, 48 D_1, 4 D_2 48 F_1, 6 F_2	16	2¼	32 C, 160 D_1, 4 D_2 160 F_1, 14 F_2	31	2¾	41 C, 200 D_1, 4 D_2 200 F_1, 16 F_2
White Prints	13	1¼	38 C, 24 E, 20 F_2	29	3	142 C, 80 E, 36 F_2	36	3½	180 C, 100 E, 40 F_2
Black Prints	10	½	48 B	32	1	160 B	40	1	200 B
Gold Prints	5	¼	7 A, 10 G	13	¼	31 A, 18 G	15	¼	40 A, 20 G
Black Border	1	1½	2 @ 2" x 48⅛" 2 @ 2" x 33¼"	1	2⅜	2 @ 2" x 77¾" 2 @ 2" x 63"	1	2⅜	4 @ 2" x 77¾"
Red Border	1	1¾	2 @ 5" x 57⅛" 2 @ 5" x 42¼"	1	2⅝	2 @ 5" x 86¾" 2 @ 5" x 72"	1	2⅝	4 @ 5" x 86¾"
(binding)		(1¾)	2 @ 1½" x 59" 2 @ 1½" x 44"		(2⅝)	2 @ 1½" x 88" 2 @ 1½" x 73½"		(2⅝)	4 @ 1½" x 88"
Lining	1	1⅞	1 @ 45" x 61"	1	5¼	2 @ 38" x 90"	1	7⅞	3 @ 30" x 90"
Batting			46" x 61"			76" x 90"			90" x 90"

AT-A-GLANCE ROTARY CUTTING OF STRIPS AND PATCHES

Fabrics	Strip Length	Strip Width	Cross Cuts	Add'l Cuts	Yield Per Strip	Number of Strips Needed Small	Med.	Large
Red Prints	9"	3½"	2 @ 3½"	--	2 C	4	16	21
	9"	4¼"	2 @ 4¼"	⊠	8 D_1	6	20	25
	9"	3"	2 @ 3"	⧄	4 D_2	1	1	1
	9"	3⅞"	2 @ 3⅞"	⧄	4 F_1	12	40	50
	9"	5½"	1 @ 5½"	⊠	4 F_2	2	4	4
White Prints	18"	3½"	5 @ 3½"	--	5 C	8	29	36
	18"	3½"	*E	*E	3 E	8	27	34
	9"	5½"	1 @ 5½"	⊠	4 F_2	5	9	10
Black Prints	18"	2"	5 @ 3½"	--	5 B	10	32	40
Gold Prints	9"	2"	4 @ 2"	--	4 A	2	8	10
	3⅜"	3⅜"	1 @ 3⅜"	⊠	4 G	3	5	5

AT-A-GLANCE

*E

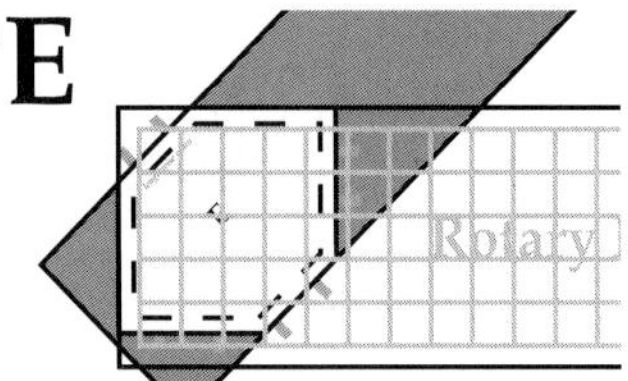

*E

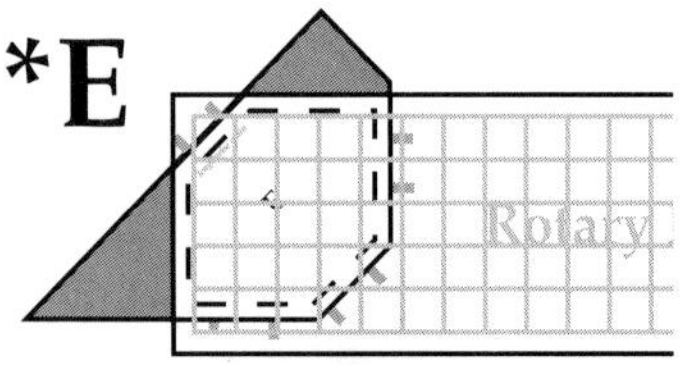

SPECIAL ROTARY CUTTING INSTRUCTIONS

⧄ For D_2 and F_1 triangles, indicated with this icon, cut lengthwise strips and cross cuts as listed to make squares. Then cut a diagonal through each square to make pairs of triangles. (Keep the fabrics layered throughout to minimize the cutting.)

⊠ For the D_1, F_2, and G triangles, indicated with this icon, cut strips and make cross cuts as listed to make squares. Then make cuts across both diagonals, leaving the stacks of triangles right next to each other after the first diagonal cut.

*E For E, cut strips 3½" wide by 18" long. Tape the E pattern to the ruler with two sides at the top and side of the ruler as shown. Align the pattern over the fabric, and cut along both edges. Turn the fabric, and cut the remaining two edges. Continue cutting E patches in this fashion down the length of the strip.

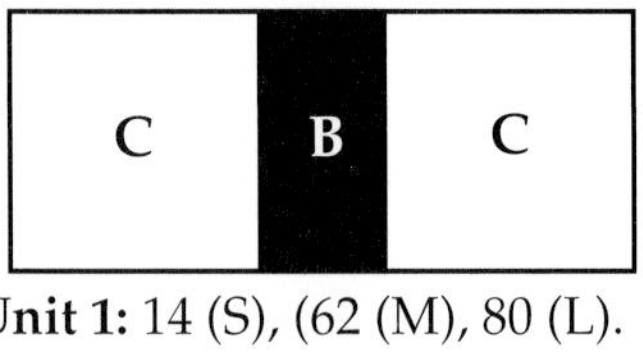

Unit 1: 14 (S), (62 (M), 80 (L).

QUILT CONSTRUCTION

1 Sew two different white print C squares to a black print B rectangle as shown to make Unit 1. Press seam allowances toward the black rectangle. Make the number listed for your size. You will have leftover B and C patches.

2 Sew two black print B rectangles to a gold print A square to make Unit 2 as shown. Press seam allowances toward the black rectangles. Repeat for each gold A to make the number required for your quilt size.

3 Sew two Unit 1's to a Unit 2 as shown, opposing seams and pinning at the joints at the ends of the rectangles. Press seams toward the Unit 2. This completes Unit 3. Repeat for each Unit 1 and Unit 2 to make the number you require.

4 Sew two red print D_1 triangles to a white print E as shown to make Unit 4. Press seams toward the red triangles. Repeat for each E to make the number listed for your quilt size.

5 Add two red print F_1 triangles to a Unit 4 to complete Unit 5 as shown. Press seam allowances toward the F_1 patches. Repeat for each Unit 4 to make the required number of units for your quilt size, as listed.

6 Sew a white print F_2 triangle to a black print B rectangle to a white print C square to make Unit 6 as shown. Press seam allowances toward the black rectangle. Repeat until you run out of C patches, making the number indicated for your quilt size.

7 Sew a gold print G triangle and a white print F_2 triangle to a black print B rectangle to complete Unit 7 as shown. Press seam allowances toward the black rectangle. Repeat for all remaining G, B, and F_2 patches to make the listed number of units.

8 Sew a Unit 6 to a Unit 7, opposing seam allowances and pinning at the joint where the two black rectangles touch. Press seam allowances toward the black B. This completes Unit 8. Repeat for each Unit 6 and Unit 7 to make the quantity indicated.

9 Refer to the quilt photograph on page 38, the small quilt drawing on page 75, and the quilt assembly diagram on page 78. Note that the rows run diagonally across the quilt. On the floor or on a design wall, lay out Units 3 and 5 plus red F_2 and D_2 triangles and C squares as follows: Start in the upper left corner of the quilt. Place a Unit 5 between two Unit 8's. Add a red D_2 in the corner. This will be the first row. Now make a row starting with a red F_2 triangle, followed by Unit 5, then a red C square, another Unit 5, and another red F_2. The third row starts with a Unit 8, followed by Unit 5-Unit 3-Unit 5-Unit 3-Unit 5 and another Unit 8.

Continue laying out units and patches according to the plan for your quilt size. Once you have laid out the entire quilt, stand back and look at it. Adjust the placement of units and patches to achieve a good color balance. In the top left corner of the leftmost unit or patch in each row, pin a paper label or stick on an adhesive office-supply label marked with the row number. Pick up and stack the units and patches in sequence, keeping them turned as they were in your layout. Place the last row patches and units on the bottom of the stack and the first row patches and units on the top of the stack. Join the patches and units into rows, referring to the diagram if needed. Press seams away from the Unit 5's. Join the rows to complete the quilt top, pinning at the corners of each unit, opposing seams. Press seam allowances away from the Unit 5's.

10 Add black borders, then add red borders, butting or mitering corners as you desire. Seam the lining panels. Press the quilt top and lining well. Mark the quilting design of your choice in the borders. Lay the lining face down, and position the batting over it. Center the quilt top, face up, over the batting and lining. Baste the layers together every four to six inches. Quilt in the ditch between all patches. Quilt the borders as marked. Bind to finish.

Unit 2
Make 7 (S), 31 (M), 40 (L).

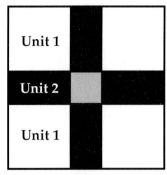

Unit 3
Make 7 (S), 31 (M), 40 (L).

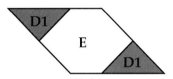

Unit 4
Make 24 (S), 80 (M), 100 (L).

Unit 5
Make 24 (S), 80 (M), 100 (L).

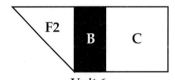

Unit 6
Make 10 (S), 18 (M), 20 (L).

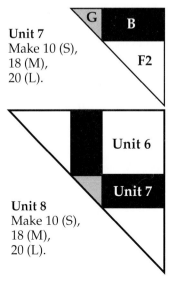

Unit 7
Make 10 (S), 18 (M), 20 (L).

Unit 8
Make 10 (S), 18 (M), 20 (L).

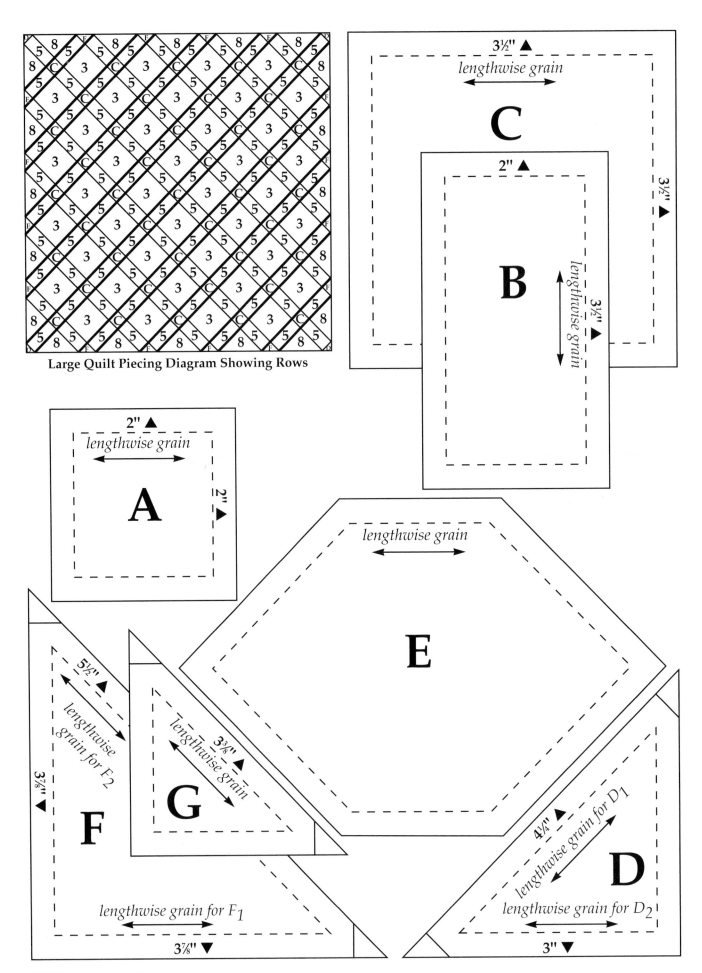

Large Quilt Piecing Diagram Showing Rows

C

3½" ▲

lengthwise grain

3½" ▲

B

2" ▲

lengthwise grain

3½"

A

2" ▲

lengthwise grain

2" ▲

E

lengthwise grain

F

5½" ▲

lengthwise grain for F₂

3⅞" ▲

lengthwise grain for F₁

3⅞" ▼

G

3⅜" ▲

lengthwise grain

D

4¼" ▲

lengthwise grain for D₁

lengthwise grain for D₂

3" ▼

SUMMERFEST

Summerfest is a simplification of the old favorite, Sister's Choice. The handsome pieced border adds a festive touch and looks impressive without adding much time and trouble to your quiltmaking. The 42" x 56" throw is shown below. The 70" x 84" twin coverlet is in the color photograph on page 39, and directions for a 96" square double spread or queen or king size coverlet are also given.

WHAT MAKES THIS QUILT EASY?

✔ There are no points to contend with around the edges of the blocks and the sawtooth borders.

✔ The ends of the cross are offset from the neighboring patches to eliminate the need for matching and to reduce bulk in the seam allowances.

✔ Among the differences between the Summerfest block and its traditional predecessor is the elimination of four patches. This means less cutting and sewing and fewer joints to match.

✔ Extending the block and border background beyond the triangles not only eliminates tricky points, but it also enlarges the blocks and borders, meaning you won't need as many blocks for a quilt.

I made Summerfest in clear, bright prints, placed randomly, and lighter solids with all four rectangles matched in a block. Because the quilt seemed busy enough with its many colors, I opted for a single cream solid for the background and a tranquil blue solid for sashes.

OTHER STUNNING COLORS

◆ Rich prints in forest, rust, burgundy, tan, teal, and eggplant; darker solids for the crosses; light gold background; and brown sashes in a paisley or floral stripe. I envision this as a warm, fall version of the summery quilt shown in the photo.

SUMMERFEST YARDAGE AND CUTTING REQUIREMENTS

Fabrics	Small - 42" x 56"			Medium - 70" x 84"			Large - 98" x 98"		
	Tot. Pcs.	Yds.	Patches	Tot. Pcs.	Yds.	Patches	Tot. Pcs.	Yds.	Patches
☐ Cream Solid	1	1½	56 B, 70 Br, 26 D, 36 F, 2 H	1	3⅜	140 B, 154 Br, 82 D, 110 F, 2 H	1	5¼	232 B, 232 Br, 146 D, 193 F, 2 H
(border)			2 @ 1½" x 44½" 2 @ 1½" x 32½"			2 @ 1½" x 72½" 2 @ 1½" x 60½"			2 @ 1½" x 88½" 2 @ 1½" x 86½"
☐ Blue Solid (border)	1	1¾	17 G 2 @ 2½" x 52½" 2 @ 2½" x 42½"	1	2⅝	49 G 2 @ 2½" x 80½" 2 @ 2½" x 70½"	1	3½	84 G 2 @ 2½" x 98½" 2 @ 2½" x 94½"
(binding)		(1¾)	2 @ 1½" x 58" 2 @ 1½" x 44"		(2⅝)	2 @ 1½" x 86" 2 @ 1½" x 72"		(3)	4 @ 1½" x 100"
☐ Bright Solids	6	½	24 E	20	1	80 E	36	2½	144 E
☐ Bright Prints	9	1	24 A, 104 C, 6 F	18	1½	80 A, 216 C, 20 F	27	1½	144A, 322 C, 36 F
Lining	1	1¾	1 @ 45" x 60"	1	2¼	2 @ 44" x 74"	1	8¾	3 @ 34" x 102"
Batting			46" x 60"			74" x 88"			102" x 102"

AT-A-GLANCE ROTARY CUTTING OF STRIPS AND PATCHES

Fabrics	Strip Length	Strip Width	Cross Cuts	Add'l Cuts	Yield Per Strip	Number of Strips Needed		
						Small	Med.	Large
Cream Solid	18"	2½"	3 @ 5¼"	*B	6 B	10	24	39
	18"	2½"	3 @ 5¼"	*Br	6 Br	12	26	39
	18"	3½"	5 @ 3½"	--	5 D	6	17	30
	18"	2½"	7 @ 2½"	--	7 F	6	16	28
	*H	*H	*H	*H	1 H	2	2	2
Blue Solid	12½"	2½"	1 @ 12½"	--	1 G	17	49	84
Bright Solids	18"	2½"	4 @ 3½"	--	4 E	6	20	36
Bright Prints	18"	2½"	2 @ 7¼"	*A	4 A	6	20	36
	18"	2⅞"	6 @ 2⅞"	◿	12 C	9	18	27
	18"	2½"	7 @ 2½"	--	7 F	1	3	6

AT-A-GLANCE

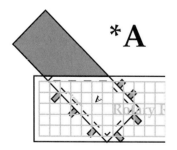

*A

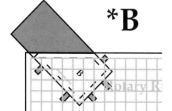

*B

SPECIAL ROTARY CUTTING INSTRUCTIONS

◿ For C triangles, indicated with this icon, cut lengthwise strips and cross cuts as listed to make squares. Then cut a diagonal through each square to make C triangles. (Keep the fabrics layered throughout to minimize the cutting.)

*A For A, cut strips 2½" x 18". Cross cut at 7¼" intervals to make rectangles. Tape the A pattern to the ruler as shown and cut the rectangles in two. Also trim the end of the remaining half of the rectangle.

*B For B, cut strips 2½" x 18". Cross cut at 5¼" intervals to make rectangles. Tape the B pattern to the ruler as shown and cut. Similarly align and cut the other half. For Br, use the B pattern and cut strips and rectangles as for B. However, turn the rectangles face down when cutting them into rhombuses.

*H For H, stack two leftover D squares. Tape the H pattern to your ruler as shown, and cut off the corner of the D's to make two H's.

QUILT CONSTRUCTION

1 Sew a cream solid Br to a bright print C to make Unit 1 as shown on page 81. Press seam allowances toward the C triangles. Make the quantity listed for your quilt size. You will have some bright print C triangles left over.

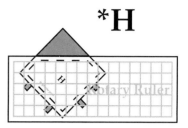

2 Sew a Unit 1 to a cream solid D square to complete Unit 2 as shown. Press seam allowances toward the D square. Make the quantity indicated for your quilt size. You will have some Unit 1's left over for the borders.

3 Sew a cream solid B to a bright print A to make Unit 3 as shown. Press seam allowances toward the bright print A patch. Make the quantity indicated. You will use all of the A's, but you will have some B's left over.

4 Sew a Unit 2 to a Unit 3 to complete Unit 4 as shown. Mix different bright prints in a Unit 4. Press the seam allowances toward the Unit 3. Repeat for all Unit 2's and 3's to make the number of Unit 4's listed for your quilt size.

5 Sew a cream solid F square to a bright solid E rectangle to complete Unit 5 as shown. Press seam allowances toward the E rectangle. Make the quantity listed. (You should have some F's left over.) Make four of these units with the same E fabric, one after the other. Then go on to the next color. When you snip apart the chains, don't snip between the four matching units. Instead, keep them chained in a group so that you can easily join them in a block later.

6 Snip off and sew a Unit 5 between two Unit 4's to complete Unit 6 as shown. Press seam allowances toward the Unit 5. Make another Unit 6 using a matching E rectangle. Then go on to make Unit 6's with a different colored E rectangle. Make the quantity listed for your quilt size. You will use all of the Unit 4's, but you will have half of the Unit 5's left. As you snip apart the Unit 6's, leave matched pairs chained together. Put the remaining two Unit 5's of the set of four with the matching pair of Unit 6's for use in the same block.

7 Snip apart and sew two matched Unit 5's to a bright print F square to make Unit 7 as shown. Press seam allowances toward the Unit 5's. Make the quantity indicated for your quilt size.

8 Sew two matching Unit 6's to a matching Unit 7 to complete Unit 8 as shown. Press seam allowances toward Unit 7. Make the quantity listed.

9 Sew a cream solid B to a bright print C to make Unit 9 as shown. Press seam allowances toward the bright print C. Make the number listed.

10 Sew a bright print C triangle to a cream solid H to make Unit 10 as shown. Press seam allowances toward the C triangle. Make two Unit 10"s.

11 See the photo on page 39 or the drawing on page 79. Lay out Unit 8's, blue solid G's, and cream solid F's in rows as follows:
   For the small quilt, you will need four sash rows alternated with 3 block rows. The small sash row has three cream F squares alternated with two blue G rectangles. The small block row has three blue G's alternated with two Unit 8's.
   For the medium quilt, you will need six sash rows and five block rows. The medium sash row has five cream F's alternated with four blue G's. The medium block row has five blue G's alternated with four Unit 8's.
   For the large quilt, you will need seven sash rows and six block rows. The large sash row has seven cream F's alternated with six blue G's. The large block row has seven blue G's alternated with six Unit 8's.
   Once you have arranged these units, adjust the placement to achieve a good color balance. Label the upper left corner of the leftmost block in each row with the row number. Pick up blocks and patches in order. Join them to make rows. Press seam allowances toward the blue G's. Join rows in order, as marked. Oppose seams and pin at the joints. After joining rows, press seams toward G's.

12 Add cream solid side borders and trim even with the quilt top. Add top and bottom borders, and trim even with sides.

13 **For the small quilt,** join 23 Unit 1's in a row. Sew to one long side of the quilt, with bright prints touching the cream border. Repeat for the opposite side. Join 16 Unit 9's in a row. Add a Unit 10 to one end and a cream D square to the other end, and stitch to the top of the quilt. Repeat for the bottom.
   For the medium quilt, join 37 Unit 1's in a row. Sew to one long side of the quilt, with bright prints touching the cream border. Repeat for the opposite side. Join 30 Unit 9's in a row. Add a Unit 10 to one end and a cream D square to the other end, and stitch to the top edge of the quilt. Repeat for the bottom edge.

Unit 1
Make 70 (S),
154 (M), 232 (L).

Unit 2
Make 24 (S),
80 (M), 144 (L).

Unit 3
Make 24 (S),
80 (M), 144 (L).

Unit 4
Make 24 (S),
80 (M), 144 (L).

Unit 5
Make 24 (S),
80 (M), 144 (L).

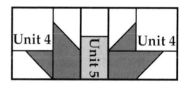

Unit 6
Make 12 (S), 40 (M), 72 (L).

Unit 7
Make 6 (S), 20 (M), 36 (L).

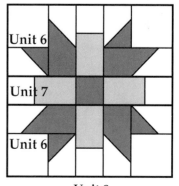

Unit 8
Make 6 (S), 20 (M), 36 (L).

Unit 9
Make 32 (S),
60 (M), 88 (L).

Unit 10
Make 2 (S),
2 (M), 2 (L).

For the large quilt, join 44 Unit 1's in a row. Sew to one side of the quilt, with bright prints touching the cream border. Repeat for the opposite side. Join 44 Unit 9's in a row. Add a Unit 10 to one end and a cream D square to the other end, and stitch to the top of the quilt. Repeat for the bottom.

14 **For all sizes,** add blue solid side borders, trimming even with quilt top. Then add top and bottom borders, trimming ends even with side borders. Seam the lining panels. Press the quilt top and lining. Mark the quilting design of your choice in the G sashes and blue borders. Lay the lining face down and position the batting over it. Center the quilt top, face up, over the batting and lining. Baste the layers together every four to six inches. Quilt in the ditch between all patches. Quilt sashes and borders as marked. Bind to finish.

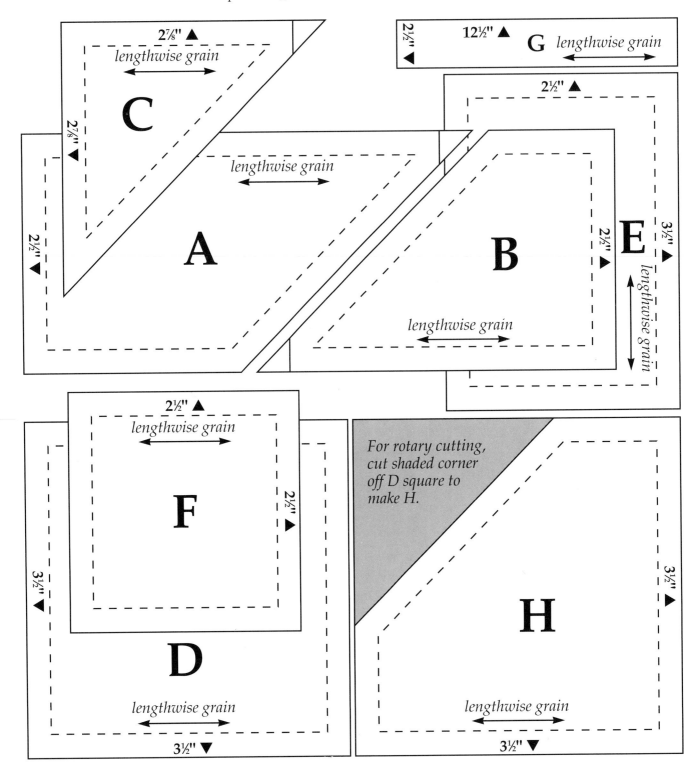

For rotary cutting, cut shaded corner off D square to make H.

RED SKY AT NIGHT

Red Sky at Night is indeed a delight in its sunset colors. This quilt improves upon the Trip Around the World pattern with an arrangement that looks complex and layered. Nevertheless, with it already mapped out for you, you'll be able to simply follow the illustrated instructions to make the quilt. The cutting and sewing couldn't be easier. In any other quilt size, this wouldn't be the same design, so I present it here in just one version, a 70" x 90" twin or double coverlet. The color photograph is on page 40.

WHAT MAKES THIS QUILT EASY?

✔ This quilt is made simply from easy-to-cut, easy-to-sew squares, with a few equally easy rectangles around the border.

✔ The quilt gets its intricate look from the arrangement of colors; the sewing is still just rows of squares, the same as for an ordinary Trip Around the World.

✔ Red Sky at Night has no stretchy bias edges and no points.

✔ Handy diagrams map out the whole quilt and take all the tricky thinking out of your quilt planning, leaving you with just straight-forward cutting and sewing.

I made Red Sky at Night in eleven fabrics--nine prints and two solids. The prints are in four gradated shades of blue and three shades of rose plus cream. A second navy blue provides an accent. The solids are in two shades of rose. The colors are numbered in the yardage chart and diagrams for easy reference.

OTHER STUNNING COLORS

◆ This quilt would look equally good in other pairs of gradated colors, such as peach and green, pink and purple, coral and turquoise, or brown and gold.

Fabrics	Size - 70" x 90" No. Pcs.	Tot. Yds.	Patches	Strip Length	Strip Width	Cross Cuts	Yield per Strip	Number of Strips Needed
1. Navy Print	1	¼	9 A	9"	2½"	3 @ 2½"	3 A	3
2. Wine Print	1	¼	42 A	9"	2½"	3 @ 2½"	3 A	14
3. Rose Print	1	½	82 A	18"	2½"	7 @ 2½"	7 A	12
4. Light Pink Print	1	1	126 A	18"	2½"	7 @ 2½"	7 A	18
5. Cream Print	1	1	166 A	18"	2½"	7 @ 2½"	7 A	24
6. Rose Solid	1	1	88 A	18"	2½"	7 @ 2½"	7 A	10*
			10 B	18"	2½"	1 @ 14½", 1 @ 2½"	1 B, 1 A*	10
			4 C	18"	2½"	2 @ 8½"	2 C	2
			4 D	18"	2½"	1 @ 10½", 2 @ 2½"	1 D, 2 A*	4
7. Navy Print	1	2¾	120 A	18"	2½"	7 @ 2½"	7 A	18
(binding)		(2¾)		92"	1½"		1 strip	4
8. Bright Blue Print	1	1	198 A	18"	2½"	7 @ 2½"	7 A	29
9. Med. Blue Print	1	1	202 A	18"	2½"	7 @ 2½"	7 A	29
10. Light Blue Print	1	½	90 A	18"	2½"	7 @ 2½"	7 A	13
11. Wine Solid	1	1⅝	204 A	18"	2½"	7 @ 2½"	7 A	28**
			4 B	18"	2½"	1 @ 14½", 1 @ 2½"	1 B, 1 A**	4
			10 E	18½"	2½"	1 @ 18½"	1 E	10
			4 F	18"	2½"	1 @ 12½", 2 @ 2½"	1 F, 2 A**	4
Lining	1	5½		94"	37"		1 panel	2 panels
Batting						74" x 94"		

AT-A-GLANCE

Unit A: Make 4.

Unit B: Make 4.

Unit C: Make 4.

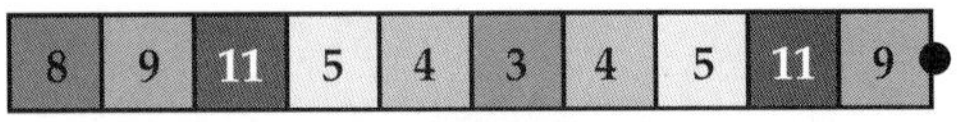

Unit D: Make 4.

Unit E: Make 16.

Unit F: Make 8.

Unit G: Make 12.

Unit H: Make 12.

Unit I: Make 12.

SPECIAL ROTARY CUTTING INSTRUCTIONS

✱✱ The number of A patches may appear to differ from the cutting requirements. Closer inspection will reveal that A patches that are indicated with * and ** are cut in combination with other patches, as well as alone, for the correct total.

QUILT CONSTRUCTION

1 Units A-Z are made from A squares of various colors joined to make rows. It is important for you to follow the color sequence closely. Each color listed in the yardage chart above is preceded by a number. This number is also used in the figures to identify the fabrics. Make a reference sheet by taping a small sample of each fabric to a piece of paper and labeling each sample with the appropriate number. You may also find it helpful to make stacks of squares, with separate piles for those cut from fabric #1, #2, and so on. Arrange the stacks in numerical order, with a label next to each stack. Once you have organized your stacks in this way, you will be able to instantly identify squares of the appropriate colors as you make the units.

The dot at one end of Units A-J marks the end of the unit that is on the inside, that is, the end that gets sewn to the center units K-Z. (K-Z are the same turned either way.) Make units A-Z in the quantities indicated. You will need one Z; two each of K, L, M, N, O, U, V, W, X, and Y; four each of A, B, C, D, P, Q, R, S, and T; six J; eight F; twelve G, H, and I; and sixteen E. Press seam allowances of Units A, C, E, H, and J *toward* the end marked with a •. Press seam allowances of Units B, D, F, G, and I *away* from the end marked with a •. Press seam allowances for K, M, O, Q,

S, U, W, Y, and Z from both ends *toward the center*. Press seam allowances for L, N, P, R, T, V, and X away from the center patch *toward both ends*.

2 Join units A-Z as shown on page 86 to make rows the full width of the quilt. The rows are numbered from 1 to 16. Remember to turn side units A-J so that the end marked with a • is stitched to the center unit. Press seam allowances at these seams the same direction as the neighboring seam allowances. You will need varying numbers of these rows: Make two each of Rows 1-5 and 11-15. Make four each of Rows 6-10. Make one of Row 16.

3 Everything in this step is repeated a second time. The instructions are clearer when I describe the whole procedure just once and tell you to repeat the whole step. However, if you would like to repeat every part as it is described, you can save some thinking and planning later. Join Rows 1-15 in sequence. Press seam allowances toward Row 1. Join Rows 6-10, and press seam allowances toward Row 6. Add this to the Row 15 end of the Rows 1-15 made earlier. This completes the top half of the quilt. Repeat for the bottom half.

4 Sew Row 16 to Row 10 at the bottom of one half of the quilt. Turn the other half of the quilt so that Row 10 is at its top. Sew this Row 10 to the remaining edge of Row 16 to complete the quilt top. Press these last two seams away from the center of the quilt.

5 Sew two bright blue print A squares to a medium blue print A to complete Unit 5 as shown. Wait to finger press seam allowances as you pin and stitch these units to the quilt top later. Make 14 Unit 5's.

6 Sew four Unit 5's alternately with three rose solid B rectangles. Sew a rose solid C rectangle to each end. Sew to one long side of the quilt, opposing seams and pinning at the joints of each Unit 5. Repeat Step 6 for the other long edge of the quilt.

7 Sew three Unit 5's alternately with two rose solid B rectangles. Sew a rose solid D rectangle to each end. Sew to the top edge of the quilt, opposing seams and pinning at the joints of each Unit 5. Repeat Step 7 for the bottom edge of the quilt.

8 Sew four medium blue print A's alternately with three wine solid E rectangles. Sew a wine solid F rectangle to each end. Sew to one long side of the quilt, opposing seams and pinning at the joints of each of the four medium blue print A's. Repeat Step 8 for the other long edge of the quilt.

9 Sew three medium blue print A's alternately with two wine solid E rectangles. Sew a wine solid B rectangle to each end. Sew to the top edge of the quilt, opposing seams and pinning at the joints of each of the three medium blue print A's. Repeat Step 9 for the bottom edge of the quilt.

10 Seam the lining panels. Press the quilt top and lining. Lay the lining face down and position the batting over it. Center the quilt top, face up, over the batting and lining. Baste the layers together every four inches or so. Quilt in the ditch between all patches. Bind to finish.

AT-A-GLANCE

11	6	7	8	9	11	10	9	8	7

Unit J: Make 6.

11	6	7	8	9	11	9	8	7	6	11

Unit K: Make 2.

6	7	8	9	11	10	11	9	8	7	6

Unit L: Make 2.

7	8	9	11	10	9	10	11	9	8	7

Unit M: Make 2.

8	9	11	10	9	8	9	10	11	9	8

Unit N: Make 2.

9	11	10	9	8	7	8	9	10	11	9

Unit O: Make 2.

11	10	9	8	7	6	7	8	9	10	11

Unit P: Make 4.

10	9	8	7	6	5	6	7	8	9	10

Unit Q: Make 4.

9	8	7	6	5	4	5	6	7	8	9

Unit R: Make 4.

8	7	6	5	4	3	4	5	6	7	8

Unit S: Make 4.

7	6	5	4	3	2	3	4	5	6	7

Unit T: Make 4.

6	5	4	3	2	11	2	3	4	5	6

Unit U: Make 2.

7	6	5	4	11	10	11	4	5	6	7

Unit V: Make 2.

8	7	6	11	10	9	10	11	6	7	8

Unit W: Make 2.

9	8	11	10	9	8	9	10	11	8	9

Unit X: Make 2.

10	11	10	9	8	7	8	9	10	11	10

Unit Y: Make 2.

6	5	4	3	2	1	2	3	4	5	6

Unit Z: Make 1.

8	9	8

Unit 5: Make 14.

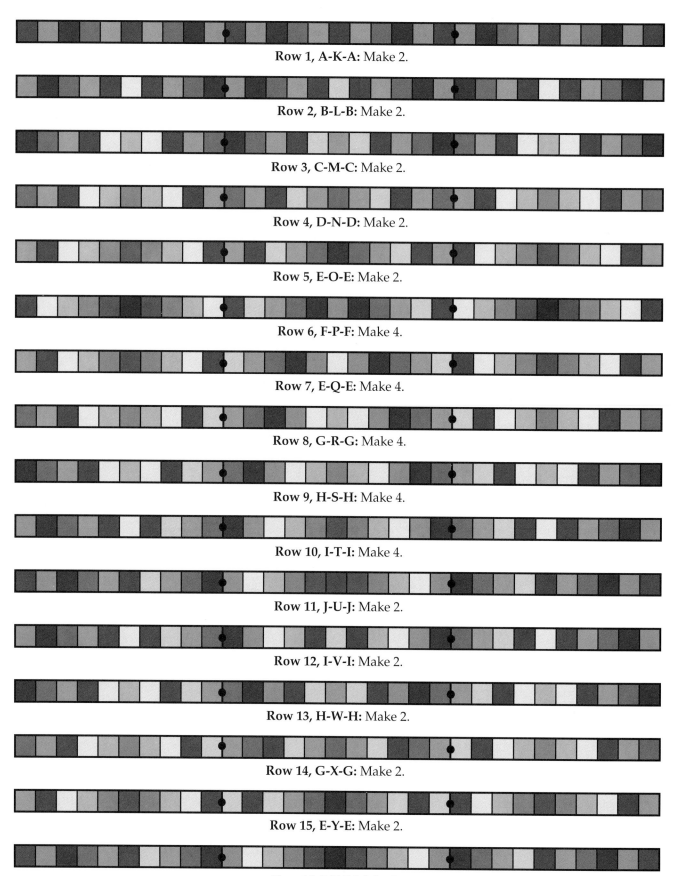

Row 1, A-K-A: Make 2.

Row 2, B-L-B: Make 2.

Row 3, C-M-C: Make 2.

Row 4, D-N-D: Make 2.

Row 5, E-O-E: Make 2.

Row 6, F-P-F: Make 4.

Row 7, E-Q-E: Make 4.

Row 8, G-R-G: Make 4.

Row 9, H-S-H: Make 4.

Row 10, I-T-I: Make 4.

Row 11, J-U-J: Make 2.

Row 12, I-V-I: Make 2.

Row 13, H-W-H: Make 2.

Row 14, G-X-G: Make 2.

Row 15, E-Y-E: Make 2.

Row 16, J-Z-J: Make 1.

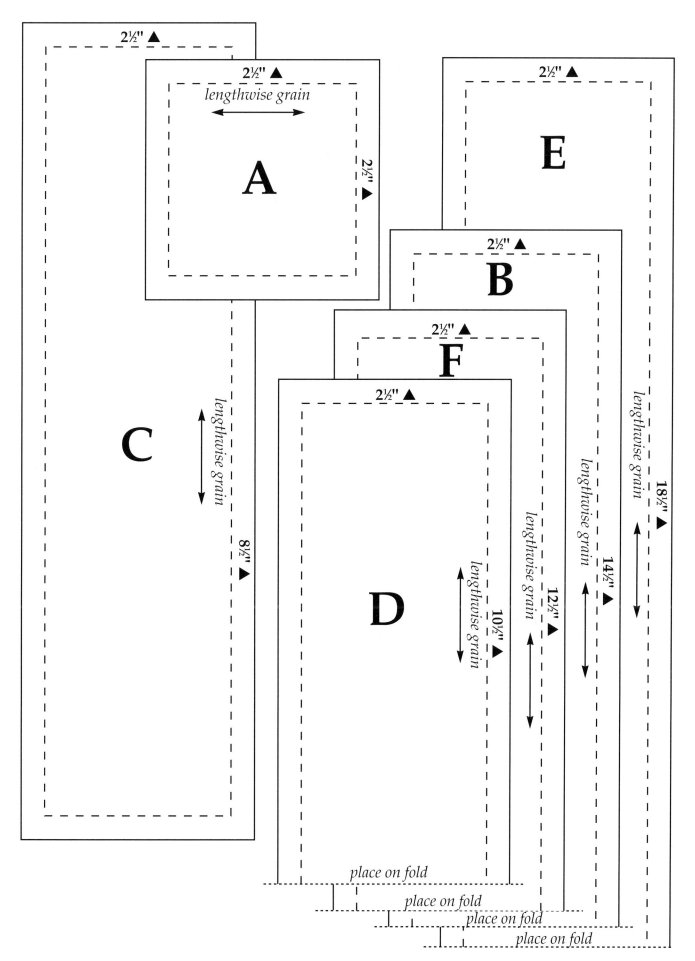

2½" ▲

2½" ▲

lengthwise grain

2½"▶

A

E

2½" ▲

2½" ▲

B

C

lengthwise grain

2½" ▲

F

8½"▶

2½" ▲

D

lengthwise grain

lengthwise grain

lengthwise grain

lengthwise grain

10½"▶

12½"▶

14½"▶

18½"▶

place on fold

place on fold

place on fold

place on fold

WIND IN MY SAILS

Wind in My Sails is a refreshing new pattern with the intricate, ordered look of a Goose in the Pond or Nebraska pattern. The blocks have many patches, but the blocks are large, and you don't need many for a quilt. The 59" wall quilt shown below has just four blocks; the 59" x 82" twin coverlet shown in color on page 41 has only six; and the 82" x 82" double or queen quilt has just nine blocks.

WHAT MAKES THIS QUILT EASY?

✔ The quilt looks complex with its small pieces, but the actual patch count is about the same as a simple Nine-Patch of 2" squares.

✔ The two-color pattern makes fabric selection quick and easy.

✔ The quilt is made from simple rotary-cut shapes joined into easy-to-sew units. There are some points and joints to work with, but you'll get an exceptionally impressive quilt for no more time and trouble than you would spend on a run-of-the-mill quilt.

I chose to make Wind in My Sails from scraps in blue and white. I'm a big fan of scraps for adding nuances of color. However, this quilt would also look attractive in just two fabrics.

OTHER STUNNING COLORS

◆ Red and natural. This could be muslin combined with red solid, red print, or red scraps. It could also be red scraps and cream scraps.

◆ A single Delft blue print with cream solid.

◆ Mixed bright prints in red, blue, pink, green, dark yellow, purple, and orange against a muslin background.

◆ Deep, rich fall colors of rust, wine, gold, brown, and forest green on beige.

◆ Medium pastels in gloriously floral, multicolored prints against ivory solid.

WIND IN MY SAILS YARDAGE AND CUTTING REQUIREMENTS

Fabrics	Small - 59" x 59" No. Pcs.	Tot. Yds.	Patches	Medium - 59" x 82" No. Pcs.	Tot. Yds.	Patches	Large - 82" x 82" No. Pcs.	Tot. Yds.	Patches
☐ Cream Solid	1	2⅝	144 A, 44 B, 16 E, 12 F, 32 G, 125 H, 8 I, 12 J, 4 K	1	3¼	204 A, 56 B, 24 E, 16 F, 48 G, 180 H, 10 I, 17 J, 6 K	1	4¾	288 A, 72 B, 36 E, 21 F, 72 G, 260 H, 12 I, 24 J, 8 K
■ Blue Prints	16	2	96 A, 28 B, 16 C, 16 D, 64 G, 100 H	24	2½	132 A, 32 B, 24 C, 24 D, 96 G, 144 H	36	3	180 A, 36 B, 36 C, 36 D, 144 G, 208 H
Blue Border	1	1⅞	4 @ 2½" x 59½"	1	2½	2 @ 2½" x 82½" 2 @ 2½" x 59½	1	2½	4 @ 2½" x 82½"
(binding)		(1⅞)	4 @ 1½" x 61"		(2½)	2 @ 1½" x 84" 2 @ 1½" x 61"		(2½)	4 @ 1½" x 84"
Lining	1	3¾	2 @ 32" x 63"	1	5⅛	2 @ 32" x 86"	1	7⅝	3 @ 29" x 86"
Batting			63" x 63"			63" x 86"			86" x 86"

AT-A-GLANCE ROTARY CUTTING OF STRIPS AND PATCHES

Fabrics	Strip Length	Strip Width	Cross Cuts	Add'l Cuts	Yield Per Strip	Number of Strips Needed Small	Med.	Large
Cream Solid	18"	2⅞"	6 @ 2⅞"	⧄	12 A	12	17	24
	18"	3⅞"	4 @ 3⅞"	⧄	8 B	6	8	11
	18"	2½"	2 @ 6½", 1 @ 2½"	--	2 E, 1 F	8	12	18
	18 "	2½"	7 @ 2½"	--	7 F	1	1	1
	18"	1½"	2 @ 6½", 3 @ 1½"	--	2 G, 3 H	16	24	36
	18"	1½"	11 @ 1½"	--	11 H	6	8	12
	18"	1½"	1 @ 14½", 2 @ 1½"	--	1 I, 2 H	8	10	12
	20½"	3½"	1 @ 20½"	--	1 J	12	17	24
	18"	3½"	5 @ 3½"	--	5 K	1	2	2
Blue Prints	18"	2⅞"	6 @ 2⅞"	⧄	12 A	8	11	15
	9"	3⅞"	2 @ 3⅞"	⧄	4 B	7	8	9
	18"	2⅝"	*C	--	2 C	8	12	18
	9"	2½"	2 @ 3½"	--	2 D	8	12	18
	18"	1½"	2 @ 6½", 3 @ 1½"	--	2 G, 3 H	32	48	72
	9"	1½"	5 @ 1½"	--	5 H	1	--	--

SPECIAL ROTARY CUTTING INSTRUCTIONS

⧄ For A and B triangles, indicated with this icon, cut lengthwise strips and cross cuts as listed to make squares. Then cut a diagonal through each square to make triangles. (Keep the fabrics layered throughout to minimize the cutting.)

*C For C, cut strips 2⅝" wide by 18" long. Tape the C pattern to your rotary ruler as shown, with the two short ends along two edges of the ruler. Align the pattern over a stack of Short Strips, and cut off the two ends to complete one C. Rotate the remainder of the fabric strip and align three sides of the pattern with the fabric. Make one cut to complete another C.

AT-A-GLANCE

*C

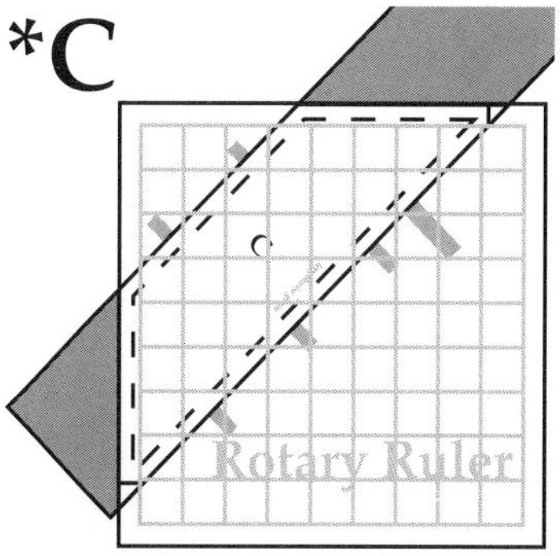

QUILT CONSTRUCTION

1 Sew two cream solid H squares to a blue print H to make Unit 1 as shown. Press seam allowances toward the blue square. Repeat to make the quantity listed for your quilt size. You will have blue and cream H squares left over after this step.

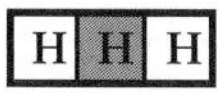

Unit 1: 50 (S), 72 (M), 104 (L).

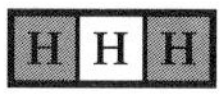

Unit 2: 25 (S), 36 (M), 52 (L).

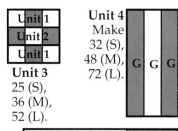

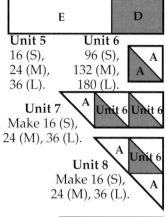

Unit 4
Make
32 (S),
48 (M),
72 (L).

Unit 3
25 (S),
36 (M),
52 (L).

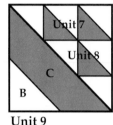

Unit 5
16 (S),
24 (M),
36 (L).

Unit 6
96 (S),
132 (M),
180 (L).

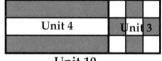

Unit 7
Make 16 (S),
24 (M), 36 (L).

Unit 8
Make 16 (S),
24 (M), 36 (L).

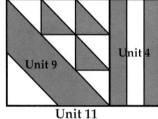

Unit 9
Make 16 (S), 24 (M), 36 (L).

Unit 10
Make 16 (S), 24 (M), 36 (L).

Unit 11
Make 16 (S), 24 (M), 36 (L).

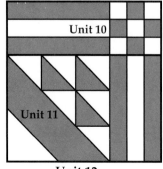

Unit 12
Make 16 (S), 24 (M), 36 (L).

2 Sew two blue print H squares to a cream solid H to make Unit 2 as shown on page 89. Press seams toward the blue squares. Repeat until you run out of cream and blue H's, to complete the number of units listed.

3 Sew two Unit 1's to a Unit 2 as shown, opposing seams and pinning at the joints between squares. Press seam allowances toward the Unit 2. This completes Unit 3. Repeat for all the Unit 1's and Unit 2's to make the quantity indicated.

4 Sew two blue print G rectangles to a cream solid G to make Unit 4 as shown. Press seam allowances toward the blue G's. Repeat for all G patches to make the number of units listed.

5 Sew a cream solid E rectangle to a blue print D rectangle as shown to make Unit 5. Press seams toward the blue D. Repeat for all D's and E's to make the number indicated.

6 Sew a blue print A triangle to a cream solid A triangle as shown to make Unit 6. Press seam allowances open; that is, press the cream seam allowances toward the cream triangles and the blue print seam allowances toward the blue triangles. Repeat for all of the blue A triangles. (You will have some cream A's left for Units 7 and 8.) Make the quantity listed for your size.

7 Join a cream A triangle and two Unit 6's as shown to make Unit 7. Press seam allowances toward the cream A triangle. Make the listed number. You will have some Unit 6's and cream A's left over for Steps 8 and 16.

8 Sew two cream A triangles to a Unit 6 to complete Unit 8 as shown. Press seam allowances away from the Unit 6. Repeat for all remaining cream A triangles to make the quantity indicated for your quilt size.

9 Sew a Unit 7 to a Unit 8 as shown. Oppose seam allowances and pin at the joint before stitching. Press seam allowances toward Unit 8. Add a blue print C patch and a cream solid B triangle as shown to make Unit 9. Press seams toward the blue C. Repeat for all Units 7 and 8 to make the quantity required for your quilt size.

10 Sew a Unit 4 to a Unit 3, opposing seams and pinning at joints. Press seam allowances toward the Unit 4. This completes Unit 10. Make the quantity listed. You will have leftover Units 3 and 4.

11 Sew a Unit 9 to a Unit 4 to complete Unit 11 as shown. Press seam allowances toward the Unit 4. Repeat for each remaining Unit 4 and each Unit 9 to make the number listed at left for your quilt size.

12 Sew a Unit 10 to a Unit 11 as shown to make Unit 12. Oppose seams and pin joints before stitching. Press seam allowances toward Unit 10. Repeat for each Unit 10 and Unit 11 to make the quantity indicated for your size.

13 Sew two Unit 12's to a Unit 5 to make Unit 13 as shown on page 91. Pin at the joint where the cream E rectangle touches the cream B triangle. Press seam allowances toward Unit 5. Repeat for all Unit 13's to make the required number for your quilt.

14 Sew two Unit 5's to a cream solid F square to make Unit 14 as shown. Press seam allowances toward the F square. Make the number listed.

15 Sew two Unit 13's to a Unit 14, pinning at joints on each end of blue D rectangles. Press seam allowances toward the Unit 14. This completes Unit 15, the quilt block. Make the quantity indicated.

16 Join six Unit 6's and a cream F as shown. Press seams away from the center. Add a cream solid I rectangle to touch the cream triangles to make Unit 16 as shown. Press seam allowances toward the cream solid I. Make the number indicated.

17 Sew a blue print B triangle to a cream B as shown. Press seams open with an iron. Repeat. Sew two of these to a Unit 16, turning them as shown to complete Unit 17. Press seams toward the B triangles. Make the number listed.

18 For the large quilt, sew four Unit 3's alternately with three cream J's to make a sash row. Make four sash rows. Sew four J's alternately with three Unit 15's to make a block row. Make three block rows. Join sash rows and block rows, alternating types. Make pieced borders as follows: Join three Unit 17's alternately with two cream K's. Make four of these pieced borders.

For the medium quilt, sew three Unit 3's alternately with two cream J's to make a sash row. Sew three J's alternately with two Unit 15's for a block row. Make four sash rows and three block rows. Join sash rows and block rows, alternating types. Make pieced side borders by joining three Unit 17's alternately with two cream K squares. Make two of these pieced side borders. Make two more pieced borders for the top and bottom of the quilt. For each of these, join two Unit 17's with a K between them.

For the small quilt, sew three Unit 3's alternately with two cream J's to make a sash row. Sew three J's alternately with two Unit 15's for a block row. Make three sash rows and two block rows. Join sash rows and block rows, alternating types. Make pieced borders by joining two Unit 17's with a cream K square between them. Make four of these pieced borders.

For all sizes, sew a cream B to a blue B to form a square. Press the seam allowances open with an iron. Make twelve of these squares. Sew one of these squares to each end of the two pieced side borders. Sew two of these squares to each end of the pieced top and bottom borders. Sew the pieced side borders to the quilt, pinning at the ends of the J patches. Then add the top and bottom pieced borders. Sew the plain blue borders to the four sides of the quilt, butting corners or mitering them as desired. (Further instructions for adding borders are on page 28.)

19 Join the lining panels with one or more lengthwise seams of ¼". Press the quilt top and lining well. Mark the quilting design of your choice in the J sashes and borders. Place the lining face down. Center the batting over it, and trim away the excess. Place the quilt top, face up, centered over the batting. Baste through all three layers, starting at the middle and working your way toward the edges in horizontal and vertical lines about 6" apart. Quilt in the ditch between patches and along border seams. Quilt the sashes and borders as marked. Bind to finish

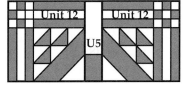

Unit 13
Make 8 (S), 12 (M), 18 (L).

Unit 14
Make 4 (S), 6 (M), 9 (L).

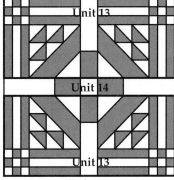

Unit 15
Make 4 (S), 6 (M), 9 (L).

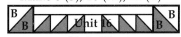

Unit 16
Make 8 (S), 10 (M), 12 (L).

Unit 17
Make 8 (S), 10 (M), 12 (L).

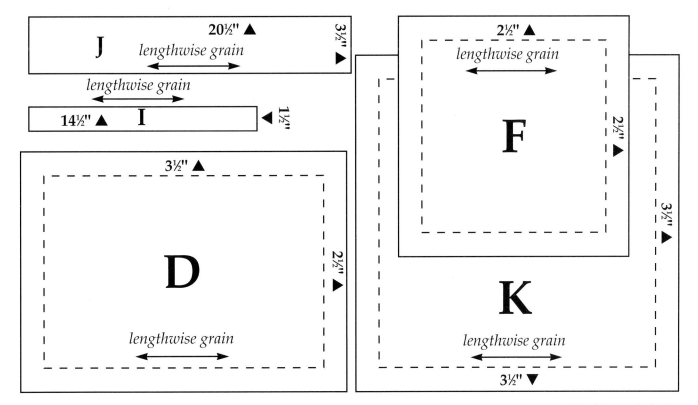

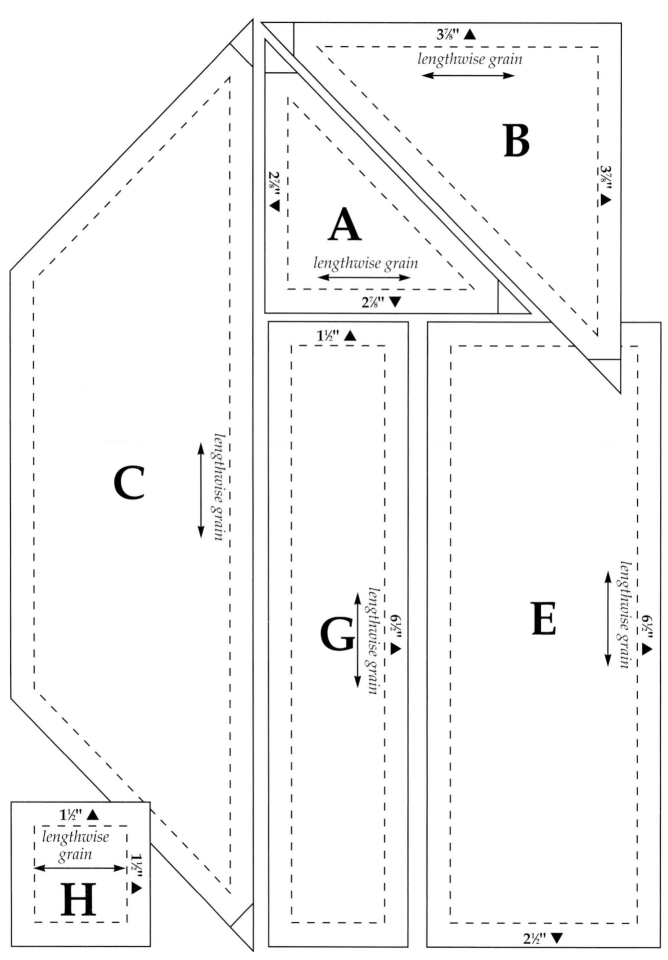

B
3⅞" ▲
lengthwise grain
3⅞" ▶

A
2⅞" ▲
2⅞" ▼
lengthwise grain

C
lengthwise grain

G
1½" ▲
6½" ▶
lengthwise grain

E
6½" ▶
lengthwise grain
2½" ▼

H
1½" ▲
1½" ▶
lengthwise grain

WEDDING MEMORIES

Wedding Memories is a perfect wedding or anniversary gift for a special couple. Interlocked wedding bands and steps to the altar combine gracefully in this design. The octagons provide ample space for signatures and messages from family and friends or they can be used to show off your fine quilting. Below is the 59" square wall quilt. On page 42 is the color photo of the 77" x 95" twin or double size quilt. Directions are also included for a 95" x 95" queen or king size.

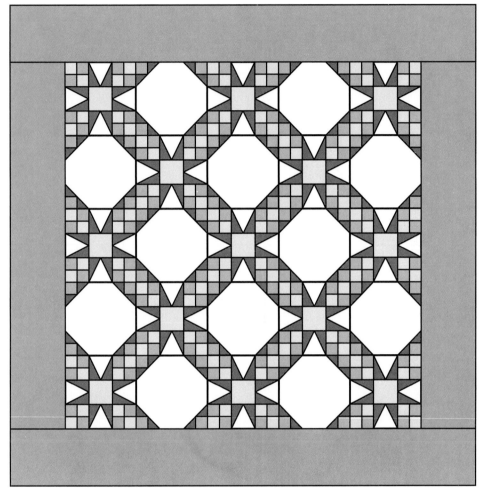

WHAT MAKES THIS QUILT EASY?

✔ The quilt gives the impression of complicated curves, as in the Wedding Rings pattern, but here the effect is achieved with simple, straight seams.

✔ The fast, accurate method for rotary cutting the dogtooth triangles in the star blocks automatically trims the points for easy alignment of patches for stitching.

✔ The borders are simply cut from a floral striped fabric, though clever positioning of the print suggests the look of intricate broderie perse.

This quilt was made in a single cream solid plus a variety of prints in creamy colors plus light and dark blues. Each of the eight star points in a block is made from the same dark blue print, and a different dark blue print is used for each block. The dark blue triangles in the octagon blocks are placed randomly.

OTHER STUNNING COLORS

◆ Ivory solid, light pink print, rose print, and maroon print. Substitute maroon for the dark blue triangles. Replace the light blue with rose and the light prints with light pink. An ivory background provides a sharp contrast.

◆ Cream background, black triangles, brown squares, and gold for the lights.

◆ Muslin background, 1930's green solid triangles, mixed bright print squares, and light squares of various colors on white backgrounds.

◆ Cream background, brown triangles, coral squares, and light pink.

◆ Aqua background, teal triangles, coral and salmon squares.

WEDDING MEMORIES YARDAGE AND CUTTING REQUIREMENTS

Fabrics	Small - 59" x 59"			Medium - 77" x 95"			Large - 95" x 95"		
	No. Pcs.	Tot. Yds.	Patches	No. Pcs.	Tot. Yds.	Patches	No. Pcs.	Tot. Yds.	Patches
☐ Cream Solid	1	1¼	52 C, 12 F	1	3⅜	128 C, 31 F	1	3⅞	164 C, 40 F
☐ Light Prints	13	½	13 A, 104 D	16	1½	32 A, 256 D	41	1½	41 A, 328 D
☐ M. Blue Prints	19	½	152 D	16	1½	380 D	31	1½	488 D
☐ Dk. Blue Prints	13	1	52 B, 52 Br, 96 E	16	1½	128 B, 128 Br, 248 E	21	2	164 B, 164 Br, 320 E
Border	1	1⅞	4 @ 7½" x 59½"	1	2⅞	2 @ 7½" x 95½" 2 @ 7½" x 77½"	1	2⅞	4 @ 7½" x 95½"
(binding)		(1⅞)	4 @ 1½" x 61"		(2⅞)	2 @ 1½" x 97" 2 @ 1½" x 79"		(2⅞)	4 @ 1½" x 97"
Lining Batting	1	3¾	2 @ 32" x 63" 63" x 63"	1	5⅞	2 @ 41" x 99" 81" x 99"	1	8¾	3 @ 33" x 99" 99" x 99"

AT-A-GLANCE ROTARY CUTTING OF STRIPS AND PATCHES

Fabrics	Strip Length	Strip Width	Cross Cuts	Add'l Cuts	Yield Per Strip	Number of Strips Needed		
						Small	Med.	Large
Cream Solid	18"	3½"	*C	*C	8 C	7	16	21
	19"	9½"	2 @ 9½"	*F	2 F	6	16	20
Light Prints	18"	3½"	5 @ 3½"	--	5 A	3	7	9
	18"	2"	8 @ 2"	--	8 D	13	32	41
M. Blue Prints	18"	2"	8 @ 2"	--	8 D	19	48	61
Dk. Blue Prints	18"	2¼"	4 @ 4⅜"	*B	8 B	7	16	21
	18"	2¼"	4 @ 4⅜"	*Br	8 Br	7	16	21
	18"	2⅜"	7 @ 2⅜"	☐	14 E	7	18	23

AT-A-GLANCE

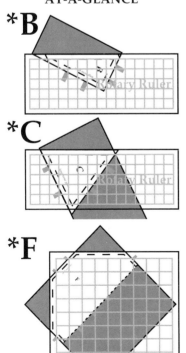

✳B

✳C

✳F

SPECIAL ROTARY CUTTING INSTRUCTIONS

☐ For the E triangles, indicated with this icon, cut lengthwise strips and cross cuts as listed to make squares. Then cut a diagonal through each square to make pairs of triangles. (Keep the fabrics layered throughout to minimize the cutting.)

✳B For B, cut strips 2¼" wide by 18" long. Make cross cuts at 4⅜" intervals to make rectangles. Tape the B pattern to your rotary ruler as shown. Align the pattern over a stack of rectangles and cut along the ruler to complete B. Align the ruler over the remaining half of the rectangle and trim the end to make another B. For Br, use the same B pattern already taped to the ruler. Cut strips and rectangles as for B, but turn the fabric rectangles face down to cut Br's.

✳C For C, cut strips 3½" wide by 18" long. Tape the C pattern to your rotary ruler as shown. Align the pattern over the stack of strips, and cut along the edge of the ruler. Turn the fabric strips face down, align the pattern with the newly cut edge, and cut again to complete one stack of C triangles. Turn the strips face up again. Align the pattern with the long sides of the fabric as well as the newly cut edge. Cut again to complete a second stack of C's. Continue cutting C's in this way, turning the ruler as needed.

✳F For F, cut strips 9½" wide by 19" long. Cut in half crosswise to make two stacks of 9½" squares. Tape the half octagon pattern from page 96 to your rotary ruler as shown, with the two longer sides of the pattern at the top and side of the ruler. Align the shorter, straight-grain sides of the pattern over a stack of squares. Cut off the two corners along the ruler. Repeat for the other half of the same stack of squares to complete a stack of octagons.

QUILT CONSTRUCTION

1 Sew two dark blue print E triangles (different fabrics) to a medium blue print D square to make Unit 1 as shown. Press seam allowances away from the D square. Make the quantity indicated for your quilt size. You will have some medium blue D squares left over. Set them aside for Step 3.

2 Sew four Unit 1's to the four long sides of an F patch to complete Unit 2 as shown. Press seam allowances away from the F. Repeat for all of the F patches to make the number listed.

3 Sew a medium blue print D square to a light print D square to make Unit 3 as shown. Press seam allowances toward the light print square. Repeat for all of the remaining D's to make the number listed.

4 Join two different Unit 3's as shown, opposing seams and pinning at the center joint. Press seam allowances toward one Unit 3. Make the number indicated for your quilt size.

5 Sew a matching dark blue B and dark blue Br to a cream solid C triangle to make Unit 5 as shown. Press seam allowances away from the C patch. Make all of the Unit 5's from one dark blue print before going on to the next print. Don't snip the threads between these matching pairs until you are ready to use them. Make the quantity listed for your quilt size.

6 Sew two matching Unit 5's to a light print A square to make Unit 6 as shown. Press seam allowances toward the A square. Set aside the remaining two matching Unit 5's for Step 7. Continue making Unit 6's from half of each set of matching Unit 5's. Make the number needed for your quilt size, as listed.

7 Sew two Unit 4's to one of the reserved Unit 5's to make a Unit 7 as shown. Be sure to turn the Unit 4's so that the medium blue print squares touch the dark blue star points. Press seam allowances toward the Unit 4's. After making two matching Unit 7's, group them with the matching Unit 6. Make the listed number of units.

8 Sew two Unit 7's to a Unit 6 to make a Unit 8 as shown. Press seam allowances toward the Unit 7's. Within a Unit 8, all B and Br triangles should be cut from the same dark blue print. Make the quantity listed.

9 On a bed or on a design wall, arrange Unit 8's and Unit 2's alternately in rows. Odd-numbered rows start with a star block (Unit 8); even-numbered rows start with an octagon block (Unit 2). **For the small quilt,** you will need five rows of five blocks each. **For the medium sized quilt,** you will need nine rows of seven blocks each. **For the large quilt,** you will need nine rows of nine blocks each. **For all sizes,** after laying out the whole quilt, stand back and look at it; adjust the block placement to achieve a good color balance. In the top left corner of the leftmost block in each row, pin a paper label or stick on an adhesive office-supply label marked with the row number. Pick up and stack the blocks in sequence, keeping them turned as they were in your layout. Place the last block of the last row on the bottom of the stack, then the next-to-last block, and so on, with the first block of the first row on the top of the stack. Join the blocks to make rows, pinning at the four joints of each block. Press seam allowances toward the Unit 2's. Join the rows to complete the quilt top, pinning at the corners of each block and at the four joints of each block, opposing seams. Press all seams toward the bottom of the quilt.

10 Add borders, butting or mitering corners as you desire. If you want to use a floral stripe to advantage, you will probably want to miter the corners. Border measurements listed are long enough for mitering. You can trim a little off the side borders if you prefer to abut them.

11 Seam the lining panels. Press the quilt top and lining. Mark the quilting design of your choice in the octagons and borders. Lay the lining face down and position the batting over it. Center the quilt top, face up, over the batting and lining. Baste the layers together every four inches or so. Quilt in the ditch between patches. Quilt the octagons and borders as marked. Bind to finish.

AT-A-GLANCE

Unit 1
Make 48 (S),
124 (M), 160 (L).

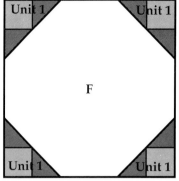

Unit 2
Make 12 (S), 31 (M), 40 (L).

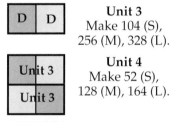

Unit 3
Make 104 (S),
256 (M), 328 (L).

Unit 4
Make 52 (S),
128 (M), 164 (L).

Unit 5
Make 52 (S),
128 (M), 164 (L).

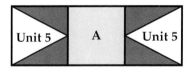

Unit 6
Make 13 (S), 32 (M), 41 (L).

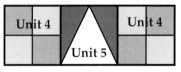

Unit 7
Make 26 (S), 64 (M), 82 (L).

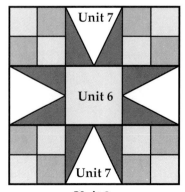

Unit 8
Make 13 (S), 32 (M), 41 (L).

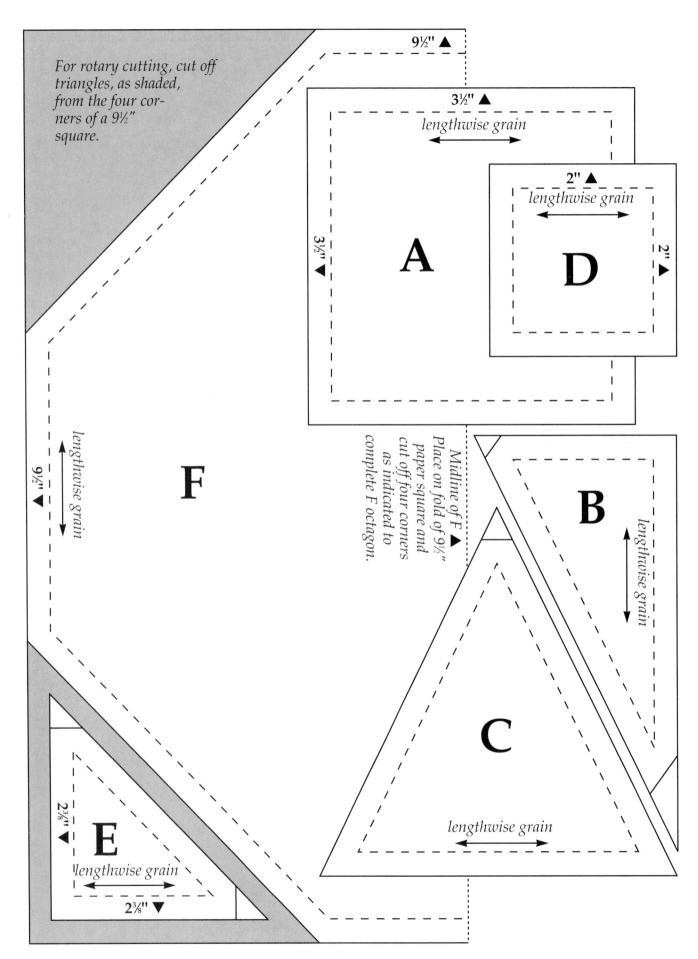

For rotary cutting, cut off triangles, as shaded, from the four corners of a 9½" square.

9½" ▲

3½" ▲

lengthwise grain

3½" ▼

A

2" ▲

lengthwise grain

2" ▶

D

9½" ◀

lengthwise grain

F

Midline of F ▶
Place on fold of 9½"
paper square and
cut off four corners
as indicated to
complete F octagon.

B

lengthwise grain

C

lengthwise grain

2⅜" ◀

E

lengthwise grain

2⅜" ▼

OLD GLORY

Old Glory sparkles with stars bursting out of a regimented arrangement. In this color scheme it suggests the American flag, although it could more resemble a flower garden in other colors. See it in color on page 43 in the 61" x 91" twin size. The 46" x 61" lap quilt is shown below. If you prefer a larger display of patriotism, make the 91" x 91" double or queen size quilt.

WHAT MAKES THIS QUILT EASY?

✔ Old Glory is made with can't-miss star points. The points don't abut sashes or other patches, making the sewing wonderfully simple.

✔ The blocks are made from simple shapes, easy to cut and easy to handle.

✔ This block minimizes matching at joints; you won't need more than two pins for any seam in the block.

I made Old Glory in red, ivory, and blue for a country look. A single navy print is used for all patches in a star, and each star is made from a different print. Because the ivory print patches touch each other, I felt it was important that they be cut from a variety of fabrics. Red and ivory solids and the red print in the sashes are the same throughout the quilt for continuity.

OTHER STUNNING COLORS

◆ Tawny prints replace both the ivory prints and ivory solid. Teal prints substitute for the navy, various brown prints for the red solid, and various black prints for the red print. The overall effect is warm, rich, and old-fashioned.

OLD GLORY YARDAGE AND CUTTING REQUIREMENTS

Fabrics	Small - 46" x 61" No. Pcs.	Tot. Yds.	Patches	Medium - 61" x 91" No. Pcs.	Tot. Yds.	Patches	Large - 91" x 91" No. Pcs.	Tot. Yds.	Patches
■ Red Solid	1	¾	96 E, 48 F	1	1½	192 E, 96 F	1	2⅛	288 E, 144 F
■ Red Print	1	½	34 I	1	½	76 I	1	1	120 I
☐ Ivory Solid	1	½	96 E, 17 F	1	1	192 E, 38 F	1	1½	288 E, 60 F
☐ Ivory Prints	16	1¾	48 C, 48 D, 48 G, 6 H	32	3¼	96 C, 96 D, 96 G, 15 H	48	4¾	144 C, 144 D, 144 G, 25 H
■ Navy Prints	12	¾	12 A, 96 B	24	1½	24 A, 192 B	36	2¼	36 A, 288 B
Border	1	1⅞	2 @ 1½" x 59½" 2 @ 1½" x 46½"	1	2¾	2 @ 1½" x 89½" 2 @ 1½" x 61½"	1	2¾	2 @ 1½" x 91½" 2 @ 1½" x 89½"
(binding)		(1⅞)	2 @ 1½" x 63" 2 @ 1½" x 48"		(2¾)	2 @ 1½" x 93" 2 @ 1½" x 63"		(2¾)	4 @ 1½" x 93"
Lining	1	3	2 @ 33" x 50"	1	5⅝	2 @ 33" x 95"	1	8⅜	3 @ 32" x 95"
Batting			50" x 65"			65" x 95"			95" x 95"

AT-A-GLANCE ROTARY CUTTING OF STRIPS AND PATCHES

Fabrics	Strip Length	Strip Width	Cross Cuts	Add'l Cuts	Yield Per Strip	Number of Strips Needed Small	Med.	Large
Red Solid	24"	1½"	4 @ 3½", 2 @ 4½"	--	4 E, 2 F	24	48	72
Red Print	18"	1½"	3 @ 5½"	--	3 I	12	26	40
Ivory Solid	18"	1½"	3 @ 3½", 1 @ 4½"	--	3 E, 1 F	17	38	60
	18"	1½"	5 @ 3½"	--	5 E	9	16	22
Ivory Prints	18"	4½"	3 @ 4½"	*C	3 C	16	32	48
	18"	3½"	5 @ 3½"	--	5 D	10	20	29
	18"	2½"	7 @ 2½"	--	7 G	7	14	21
	9"	1½"	5 @ 1½"	--	5 H	2	3	5
Navy Prints	9"	4½"	1 @ 4½"	--	1 A	12	24	36
	9"	2⅞"	2 @ 2⅞"	◿	4 B	24	48	72

AT-A-GLANCE

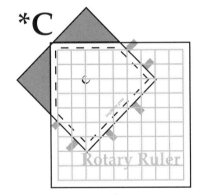

*C

SPECIAL ROTARY CUTTING INSTRUCTIONS

◿   For B triangles, indicated with this icon, cut lengthwise strips and cross cuts as listed to make squares. Then cut a diagonal through each square to make pairs of triangles. (Keep the fabrics layered throughout to minimize the cutting.)

*C   For C, cut strips 4½" wide by 18" long. Cut stacks of these strips crosswise at 4½" intervals to make stacks of squares. Tape the C pattern to your rotary ruler as shown. Align three sides of the pattern with a stack of squares. Cut along the two edges of the ruler to complete a stack of C patches.

QUILT CONSTRUCTION

Unit 1
Make 96 (S).
Make 192 (M).
Make 288 (L).

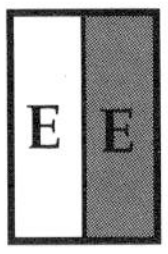

1 Sew an ivory solid E rectangle to a red solid E as shown to make Unit 1. Press seam allowances toward the red solid. Use all of the E patches to make the quantity indicated for your chosen quilt size.

2 Set aside half of the Unit 1's for Step 3. To one of the remaining Unit 1's add an ivory print G square as shown to complete Unit 2. Press seam allowances toward the G square. Make the number listed for your chosen size.

3 To one of the Unit 1's set aside previously, add an ivory print D square to complete Unit 3 as shown. Press seam allowances toward the D square. Make the number indicated. You should have no Unit 1's left at this point.

4 Join a Unit 2 and a Unit 3 as shown to make Unit 4. Press seam allowances toward the Unit 2. Use all of the Units 2 and 3 to make the number indicated for your quilt size.

5 Sew two matching navy B triangles and a red solid F rectangle to a cream print C patch as shown to make Unit 5. Press seam allowances away from the C patch. Make all four Unit 5's using the same navy print and different ivory prints. Then go on to make sets of four Unit 5's with another navy print. Make the number of units indicated for your quilt size. Leave matching units chained together and paired with the A square cut from the same navy print until you are ready to use them.

6 Sew two Unit 4's to a Unit 5 as shown to make Unit 6. Press seam allowances toward the Unit 4's. Repeat with a matching Unit 5. Set aside the other two matching Unit 5's for Step 7. Continue in this manner, using two of each set of four matching Unit 5's to make the listed number of Unit 6's.

7 Sew the two remaining matched Unit 5's of a set to a matching A square to make Unit 7 as shown. Press seam allowances toward the A square. Make the quantity indicated, using all of the remaining Unit 5's.

8 Sew two matched Unit 6's to a matching Unit 7 to make Unit 8 as shown. Press seam allowances toward the Unit 6's. This completes the quilt block. Make the number listed at the right for your quilt size.

9 Sew two red print I rectangles to an ivory solid F to complete Unit 9 as shown. Press seam allowances toward the ivory solid rectangles. This is the sash. Make the quantity listed for your quilt size.

10 Refer to the color photograph on page 43 or the drawing on page 97. On the floor or on a design wall, lay out blocks (Unit 8's), sashes (Unit 9's), and setting squares (ivory print H's) in rows as follows:

For the small quilt, you will need four block rows alternated with 3 sash rows. The small block row has three blocks alternated with two sashes. The small sash row has three sashes alternated with two ivory print H squares.

For the medium quilt, you will need six block rows and five sash rows. The medium block row has four blocks alternated with three sashes. The medium sash row has four sashes alternated with three ivory print H's.

For the large quilt, you will need six block rows and five sash rows. The large block row has six blocks alternated with five sashes. The large sash row has six sashes alternated with five ivory print H's.

For all sizes, once you have arranged the blocks, sashes, and setting squares, stand back and look the quilt over. Adjust the block placement to achieve a good color balance. Label the upper left corner of the leftmost block in each row with the row number. Pick up blocks, sashes, and patches, stacking them in order. Join them to make sash rows and block rows. Press seam allowances toward the sashes. Join rows, alternating block rows and sash rows. Oppose seams and pin at the joints at the corners of the blocks and the F rectangles. After joining rows, press seam allowances toward the sashes.

11 Add navy side borders and trim even with the quilt top. Add top and bottom borders, and trim even with sides.

12 Seam the lining panels. Press the quilt top and lining. Lay the lining face down, and position the batting over it. Then center the quilt top, face up, over the batting and lining. Baste the layers together every four to six inches. Quilt in the ditch between all patches. Bind to finish.

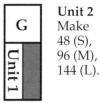

Unit 2
Make
48 (S),
96 (M),
144 (L).

Unit 3
Make
48 (S),
96 (M),
144 (L).

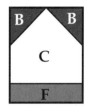

Unit 4
Make 48 (S),
96 (M),
144 (L).

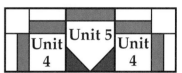

Unit 5
Make 48 (S),
96 (M),
144 (L).

Unit 6
Make 24 (S), 48 (M), 72 (L).

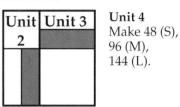

Unit 7
Make 12 (S), 24 (M), 36 (L).

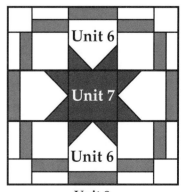

Unit 8
Make 12 (S), 24 (M), 36 (L).

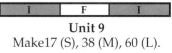

Unit 9
Make 17 (S), 38 (M), 60 (L).

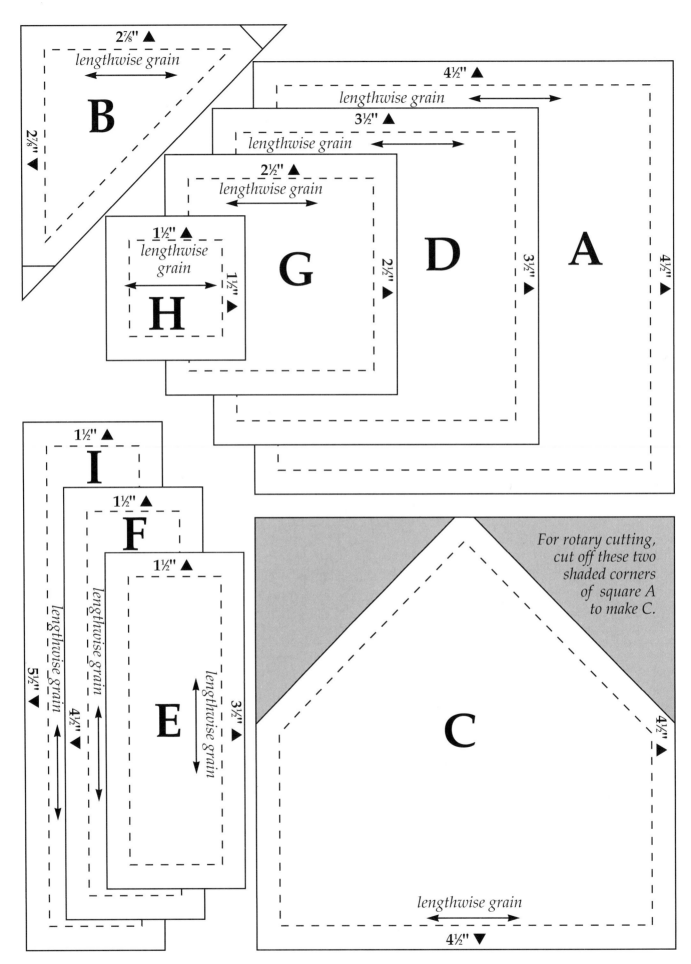

2⅞" ▲
lengthwise grain
B
2⅞" ◄

4½" ▲
lengthwise grain
3½" ▲
lengthwise grain
2½" ▲
lengthwise grain
1½" ▲
lengthwise grain
H
1½" ►
G
2½" ►
D
3½" ►
A
4½" ►

1½" ▲
I
1½" ▲
F
1½" ▲
lengthwise grain
lengthwise grain
lengthwise grain
E
5½" ▼
4½" ►
3½" ►

For rotary cutting,
cut off these two
shaded corners
of square A
to make C.
C
4½" ►
lengthwise grain
4½" ▼

COBBLESTONES

Cobblestones has the look of an antique quilt in the Strippie style. This quilt is much easier than most, and it's fun to see how different this pattern looks with different striped fabrics. You might want to make more than one. Make the 44" x 58" lap quilt shown below in no time at all. Or make the 68" x 88" twin quilt shown in the photo on page 44. A double or queen version measuring 92" x 94" is also presented.

WHAT MAKES THIS QUILT EASY?

✔ There are no triangles around the edges of the Nine-Patches and no fussy points to match.

✔ The quilt is constructed mainly of squares, and the joints are the simplest kind.

✔ The rhombus-shaped background patches are easily cut with rotary methods, and the straight grain on their outside edges makes handling easy.

✔ Sashes in the vertical plane only eliminates joints and makes this quilt exceptionally easy to set together.

✔ Wide print borders keep the piecing and quilting to a minimum.

My Cobblestones quilt was made in colors drawn from the border stripe fabric. Dark prints from eggplant to teal and rust form the crosses, with coordinating lighter prints for the center squares. I used a wide range of cream, gray, and beige prints for the background.

OTHER STUNNING COLORS

◆ Turkey red, navy, and brown crosses with scarlet, blue, and tan centers and parchment background. I envision a blue, red and tan stripe that would set off this quilt perfectly.

COBBLESTONES YARDAGE AND CUTTING REQUIREMENTS									
	Small - 44" x 58"			Medium - 68" x 88"			Large - 92" x 94"		
Fabrics	No. Pcs.	Tot. Yds.	Patches	No. Pcs.	Tot. Yds.	Patches	No. Pcs.	Tot. Yds.	Patches
☐ Cream Prints	13	1½	18 A, 78 B, 6 Br, 6 C, 6 D	19	3½	55 A, 230 B, 10 Br, 10 C, 10 D	31	5	84 A, 350 B, 14 Br, 14 C, 14 D
Dark Prints	11	1	84 A	30	2	240 A	31	3	364 A
Medium Prints	7	¼	21 A	20	½	60 A	31	½	91 A
Border Stripe	1	1¾	2 @ 7" x 58½"	1	4⅝	2 @ 7" x 88½"	1	5½	2 @ 7" x 94½"
			2 @ 7" x 44½"			2 @ 7" x 68½"			2 @ 7" x 92½"
			2 @ 2½" x 45½"			2 @ 3½" x 75½"			4 @ 3½" x 81½
						2 @ 2½" x 75½"			2 @ 2½" x 81½"
(binding)		(1¾)	2 @ 1½" x 60"		(2⅝)	2 @ 1½" x 90"		(2⅞)	2 @ 1½" x 96"
			2 @ 1½" x 46"			2 @ 1½" x 70"			2 @ 1½" x 94"
Lining	1	1½	2 @ 32" x 48"	1	5⅜	2 @ 37" x 92"	1	8⅝	3 @ 33" x 98"
Batting			48" x 62"			72" x 92"			96" x 100"

AT-A-GLANCE ROTARY CUTTING OF STRIPS AND PATCHES								
						Number of Strips Needed		
Fabrics	Strip Length	Strip Width	Cross Cuts	Add'l Cuts	Yield Per Strip	Small	Med.	Large
Cream Prints	9"	2⅝"	3 @ 2⅝"	--	3 A	6	19	28
	18"	5½"	45°, 3 @ 2⅝"	*B	6 B	13	39	59
	18"	5½"	45°, 3 @ 2⅝"	*Br	6 Br	2	3	4
	18"	5⅜"	3 @ 5⅜"	⧄	6 C	1	2	3
	*D	*D	*D	*D	1 D	6	10	14
Dark Prints	18"	2⅝"	4 @ 2⅝"	--	4 A	21	60	91
Medium Prints	9"	2⅝"	3 @ 2⅝"	--	3 A	7	20	31

AT-A-GLANCE

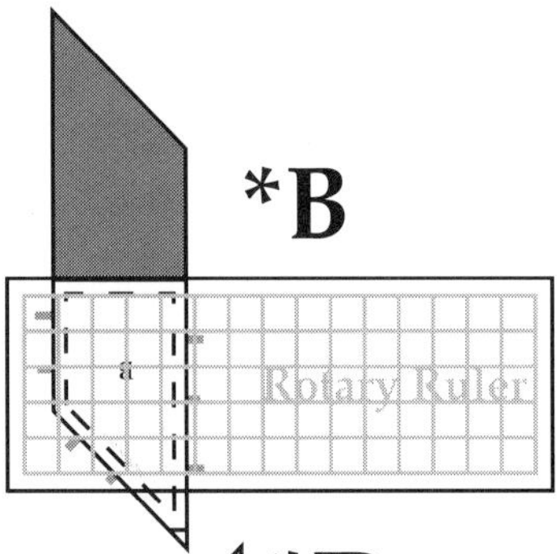

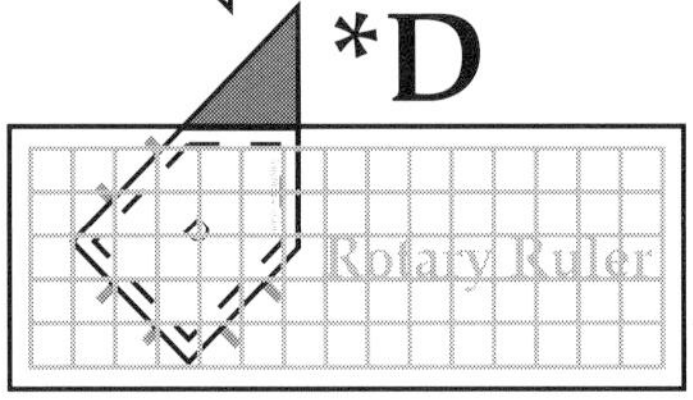

SPECIAL ROTARY CUTTING INSTRUCTIONS

⧄ For the C triangles, indicated with this icon, cut lengthwise strips and cross cuts as listed to make squares. Then cut a diagonal through each square. (Keep the fabrics layered throughout to minimize the cutting.)

*B For B, cut strips 5½" wide and 18" long in the quantities indicated. Cut off the upper right corner of a strip at a 45° angle. Align the 2⅝" line on your ruler with this cut edge of the strip. Cut three pieces at 2⅝" intervals. Trace and tape a B pattern to the underside of your rotary ruler as shown. Align a stack of fabric pieces with three edges of the pattern, and cut along the edge of the ruler to make a stack of B's. Rotate the remaining half to align it with the pattern, and trim along the ruler for another stack of B's. For Br, cut strips the same as for B. Cut off the lower right corner at a 45° angle. Cut three pieces at 2⅝" intervals. Turn these pieces face down to align with the B pattern already taped to the ruler, and cut along the edge of ruler to complete Br.

*D For D, start with four leftover B's or Br's, neatly stacked. Place B's face up and Br's face down. Trace and tape a D pattern to the underside of your rotary ruler as shown. Align the square end of the stack of B's and Br's with the D pattern. Cut off the point of the B's and Br's along the edge of the ruler to complete four D's.

1 Stack four matching dark print A squares, and pair each stack with a coordinating medium print A. Put the medium print square in the middle of the stack. Each of these stacks represents a cross in the quilt. **The small quilt** has three columns of seven crosses each. Arrange your stacks in three columns of seven stacks. **For the medium quilt,** arrange your stacks in five columns of twelve. **For the large quilt,** arrange your stacks in seven columns of thirteen.

Adjust the placement of stacks to achieve a good color balance. Separate the stacks into columns, and pin or stick on a label to the first stack in each column to indicate the column number. Next, label each stack in the column, indicating its cross number. (For example the first stack in the column would be labeled "Cross #1.") Pile the stacks for each column in sequence, with the one marked "Cross #1" on top. You will use the patches in the order they are piled, with the addition of cream patches, as indicated. Now you can start piecing columns.

Find the Unit 5 diagram for your chosen quilt size below right or on page 104. These figures show color placement as well as units. The numbers in the squares correspond to the cross numbers on your stacks. The numbers in the background patches refer to the construction units. Set aside the first four squares, three dark A's and one medium A, from the first cross of each column for Units 3 and 4.

For Unit 1, start at the top right of the figure and work toward the bottom left. Sew a cream B to the first dark print A to a cream A to the next dark print A to a cream B as shown at right. Press seam allowances toward the dark print A's.

2 Sew a cream B to the next dark print A to a medium print A to a dark print A to another cream B as shown to make Unit 2. Press seam allowances toward the dark print A patches.

Rather than making all of the units at once, you may prefer to alternate making Units 1 and 2, to correspond to the way the units will appear in the column. To do so, chain piece the first pair of patches for Unit 1, the cream B and dark print A. Then join the cream B and dark print A for Unit 2. Snip off the Unit 1 segment from the thread chain. Add a cream A square. Snip off the Unit 2 segment and add a medium print A square to it. Snip off the Unit 1 segment. Add a dark print A. Snip off the Unit 2 segment and add a dark print A. Snip off the Unit 1 segment and add a cream B. Finally, snip off the Unit 2 segment and add a cream B. This completes one Unit 1 and one Unit 2. You can join the units as you go along, or you can make all of the units before joining them.

3 Units 3 and 4 are found only at the top and bottom of each column. For the units at the top of the column, use the dark and medium A patches set aside earlier. Sew a cream D to a dark print A to a medium print A to a dark print A to a cream B to complete Unit 3. Press seam allowances toward the dark A's.

4 Sew a cream Br to a dark print A to a cream B to make Unit 3 as shown. Press seam allowances toward the dark print A patches.

5 Find the Unit 5 diagram for your chosen quilt size at right or on page 104. Join C patches and Units 1, 2, 3, and 4 in the sequence shown in the diagram to make a column. Make the number of columns required for your chosen quilt size. Press seam allowances toward the bottom right of the column.

6 **For the small quilt,** sew three patchwork columns alternately with two 2½"-wide strips. **For the medium quilt,** sew five columns alternately with four strips. The two outermost strips are the wider, 3½" strips. **For the large quilt,** sew seven columns alternately with six strips. The strips flanking the center column and the two outer columns are the wider, 3½" strips. **For all sizes,** press seam allowances toward the long strips. If you like, for the medium and large versions, you can cut the strips from different parts of the print. Feel free to change the strip widths to suit your border print. If you do change strip widths, be sure to allow for the change in length of the wide top and bottom borders.

7 Add borders, butting or mitering corners as you desire. Join the lining panels. Press the quilt top and lining. Mark the quilting design of your choice in the borders. Lay the lining face down, and center the batting and quilt top, face up, over it. Baste the layers together every six inches or so. Quilt in the ditch between all patches. Quilt the borders as marked. Bind to finish.

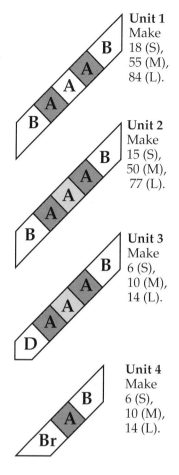

Unit 1
Make
18 (S),
55 (M),
84 (L).

Unit 2
Make
15 (S),
50 (M),
77 (L).

Unit 3
Make
6 (S),
10 (M),
14 (L).

Unit 4
Make
6 (S),
10 (M),
14 (L).

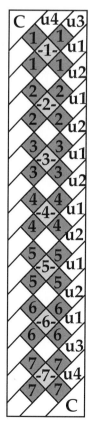

Unit 5
Make
3 (S).

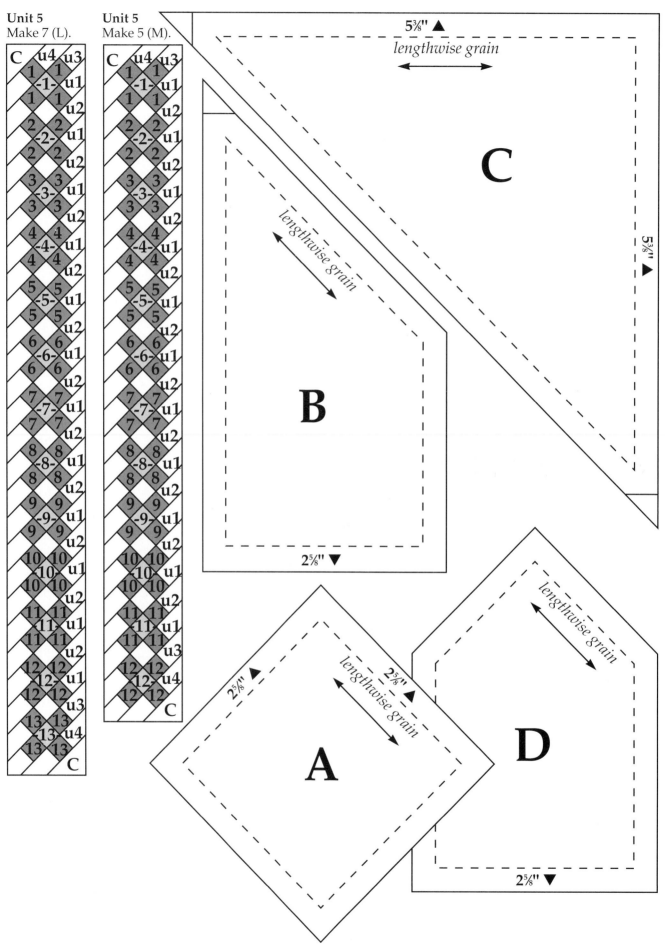

Unit 5
Make 7 (L).

Unit 5
Make 5 (M).

5⅜" ▲

lengthwise grain

C

5⅜" ▶

lengthwise grain

B

2⅝" ▼

lengthwise grain

2⅝" ▲

lengthwise grain

2⅝" ▲

lengthwise grain

A

D

2⅝" ▼

104 Cobblestones

HUDSON BAY LOG CABIN

Hudson Bay Log Cabin is a new design that fits right in with the quiltmaking tradition. Like a fieldstone chimney on a rustic log cabin, the square patches in this quilt add a delightful change of texture. This is the perfect pattern for showing off your collected fabrics. Below is the 58" x 74" throw size quilt in a Barnraising set. The 74" x 90" twin quilt photographed on page 45 is arranged in a Streak o' Lightning set. Directions for a 90" x 90" double or queen size are also included. Feel free to arrange your blocks in any Log Cabin set you desire.

WHAT MAKES THIS QUILT EASY?

✔ This quilt looks extra-special with its intriguing mix of squares and logs, but it is just as easy to make as an ordinary Log Cabin quilt.

✔ No points, no stretchy bias edges; just quick-to-cut-and-sew squares and rectangles.

✔ This, like most Log Cabins, has the simplest of joints, with only one or two pins needed for each seam in the block.

My Hudson Bay Log Cabin was made using a single wine solid, a variety of dark prints in blue, red, brown, rust, and green and light prints in buff, tan, green, beige, cream, and gold.

OTHER STUNNING COLORS

◆ Bright red solid replaces wine, bright prints in blue, green, purple, orange, pink, and turquoise substitute for the darks and light and pastel prints in baby blue, mint green, lavender, peach, pale pink, and aqua substitute for the lights.

HUDSON BAY LOG CABIN YARDAGE AND CUTTING REQUIREMENTS

Fabrics	Small - 58" x 74" No. Pcs.	Small Tot. Yds.	Small Patches	Medium - 74" x 90" No. Pcs.	Medium Tot. Yds.	Medium Patches	Large - 90" x 90" No. Pcs.	Large Tot. Yds.	Large Patches
■ Wine Solid	1	1	384 A	1	1½	640 A	1	1½	800 A
▨ Dark Prints	24	2	48 A, 48 B, 48 C, 48 D, 48 E, 48 F, 48 G	40	3	80 A, 80 B, 80 C, 80 D, 80 E, 80 F, 80 G	50	4	100 A, 100 B, 100 C, 100 D, 100 E, 100 F, 100 G
☐ Light Prints	26	2	192 A, 288 H	44	3	320 A, 480 H	53	3½	400 A, 600 H
■ Border	1	2¼	2 @ 5½" x 74½" 2 @ 5½" x 58½"	1	2¾	2 @ 5½" x 90½" 2 @ 5½" x 74½"	1	2¾	4 @ 5½" x 90½"
(binding)		(2¼)	2 @ 1½" x 76" 2 @ 1½" x 60"		(2¾)	2 @ 1½" x 92" 2 @ 1½" x 76"		(2¾)	4 @ 1½" x 92"
Lining	1	3⅝	2 @ 39½" x 62"	1	5½	2 @ 39½" x 94"	1	8¼	3 @ 32" x 94"
Batting			62" x 78"			78" x 94"			94" x 94"

AT-A-GLANCE ROTARY CUTTING OF STRIPS AND PATCHES

Fabrics	Strip Length	Strip Width	Cross Cuts	Yield Per Strip	Number of Strips Needed Small	Med.	Large
Wine Solid	18"	1½"	11 @ 1½"	11 A	35	59	73
Dark Prints	18"	1½"	1 @ 1½", 1 @ 6½", 1 @ 7½"	1 A, 1 F, 1 G	48	80	100
	18"	1½"	1 @ 2½", 1 @ 3½", 1 @ 4½", 1 @ 5½"	1 B, 1 C, 1 D, 1 E	48	80	100
Light Prints	18"	1½"	11 @ 1½"	11 A	18	30	37
	18"	2½"	7 @ 2½"	7 H	42	69	86

AT-A-GLANCE

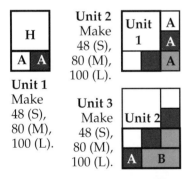

Unit 1
Make
48 (S),
80 (M),
100 (L).

Unit 2
Make
48 (S),
80 (M),
100 (L).

Unit 3
Make
48 (S),
80 (M),
100 (L).

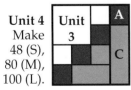

Unit 4
Make
48 (S),
80 (M),
100 (L).

Unit 5
Make
48 (S),
80 (M),
100 (L).

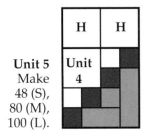

QUILT CONSTRUCTION

1 Sew a light print A square to a wine solid A square. Press seam allowances toward the wine square. Sew this A-A segment to a light print H square, as shown, to make Unit 1. Press seam allowances toward the A squares. Make the quantity listed for your quilt size. You will have light A's and H's and wine A's left over.

2 Sew a wine solid A square between a light print A and a dark print A. Press seam allowances toward the light end of this segment. Sew this segment to Unit 1 as shown to complete Unit 2. Press seam allowances away from Unit 1. Make the quantity listed for your quilt size. You will have used all of the dark print A's by now, but you will have leftover wine and light print A's.

3 Sew a wine solid A to a dark print B. Press seam allowances toward the wine square. Sew the A-B segment to a Unit 2 to make Unit 3 as shown, pinning at the joint and opposing seam allowances. Press seam allowances toward the dark print B. Make the quantity listed for your quilt size, repeating this step for each Unit 2.

4 The B and C patches of a block are cut from the same fabric. Select a C to match the B in your Unit 3. Sew a wine solid A to this dark print C. Sew the matching A-C segment to Unit 3 to complete Unit 4 as shown. Oppose seams and pin at the joint. Press seams toward the C patch. Repeat for each Unit 3 to make the number of Unit 4's listed for your quilt size.

5 Sew two light print H squares together. Press seam allowances toward the left. Add the pair of H's to a Unit 4 as shown to make Unit 5. Press the seam allowances toward the two new H patches. Repeat for each Unit 4 to make the quantity listed.

6 Join three light print H's end to end. Press seams toward the center H. Sew this segment to Unit 5 as shown to make Unit 6, pinning at the corners of the squares and opposing seams at the joints. Press the seam allowances toward the three H's. Repeat for all Unit 5's to make the quantity listed.

7 See Unit 7. Sew a wine solid A to a dark print D. Add a light print A as shown. Press seam allowances away from the wine square. To complete Unit 7 as shown, sew the A-A-D segment to a Unit 6, pinning at the joint where the wine A's touch. Press seam allowances toward the D. Repeat for each Unit 6 to make the number required for your quilt size.

8 Refer to Unit 8. The D and E patches are cut from the same fabric. Find an E to match the D in your Unit 7. Sew a wine solid A to this dark print E. Add a light print A to the wine end. Press seam allowances away from the wine square. Sew the matching A-A-E segment to Unit 7 to complete Unit 8 as shown. Press seam allowances toward the E rectangle. Repeat Step 8 for each Unit 7 to make the quantity listed for your quilt size.

9 Sew a wine solid A to a dark print F. Press seam allowances away from the wine square. To complete Unit 9 as shown, sew the A-F segment to a Unit 8, pinning at the joint where the wine squares meet. Press seam allowances toward the F. Repeat for each Unit 8 to make the number of Unit 9's listed for your quilt size.

10 F and G patches in a block are cut from the same fabric. Find a G patch to match the F in your Unit 9. Sew a wine solid A to this dark print G. Press seams away from the wine A. Sew the matching A-G segment to Unit 9 to complete Unit 10 as shown, pinning at the joint. Press seam allowances toward the G rectangle. This completes the quilt block. Repeat for each Unit 9 to make the appropriate number of units for your quilt size.

11 On the floor or on a design wall, arrange the blocks in rows. **For the small quilt,** you will need eight rows of six blocks each. **For the medium quilt,** you will need ten rows of eight blocks each. **For the large quilt,** you will need ten rows of ten blocks each. Study the quilt photograph on page 45 and the drawing on page 105 to see how different effects can be achieved by turning the blocks different ways. Decide on an arrangement, and place blocks accordingly. Adjust block placement to achieve a good color balance. In the top left corner of the leftmost block in each row, pin a paper label or stick on an adhesive office-supply label marked with the row number. Pick up and stack the blocks of each row in sequence, keeping them turned as they were in your layout. Place the last block on the bottom of the stack, then the next-to-last block, and so on, with the first block on the top of the stack. Join the blocks to make rows, referring to the diagram or photograph if needed. Press seam allowances for odd-numbered rows to the right and for even-numbered rows to the left. Join the rows to complete the quilt top. Pin at the corners of each block, opposing seams. Press row seam allowances toward the bottom of the quilt.

13 Add the borders, mitering the corners. Seam the lining panels. Press the quilt top and lining well. Mark the quilting design of your choice in the borders. Lay the lining face down, and place the batting over it. Then center the quilt top, face up, over the batting and lining. Baste the layers together every four to six inches. Quilt in the ditch between all patches. Quilt the borders as marked. Bind to finish.

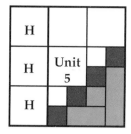

Unit 6
Make
48 (S),
80 (M),
100 (L).

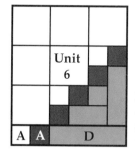

Unit 7
Make
48 (S),
80 (M),
100 (L).

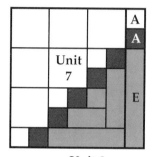

Unit 8
Make 48 (S), 80 (M), 100 (L).

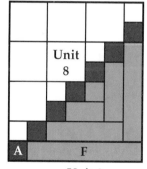

Unit 9
Make 48 (S), 80 (M), 100 (L).

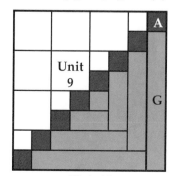

Unit 10
Make 48 (S), 80 (M), 100 (L).

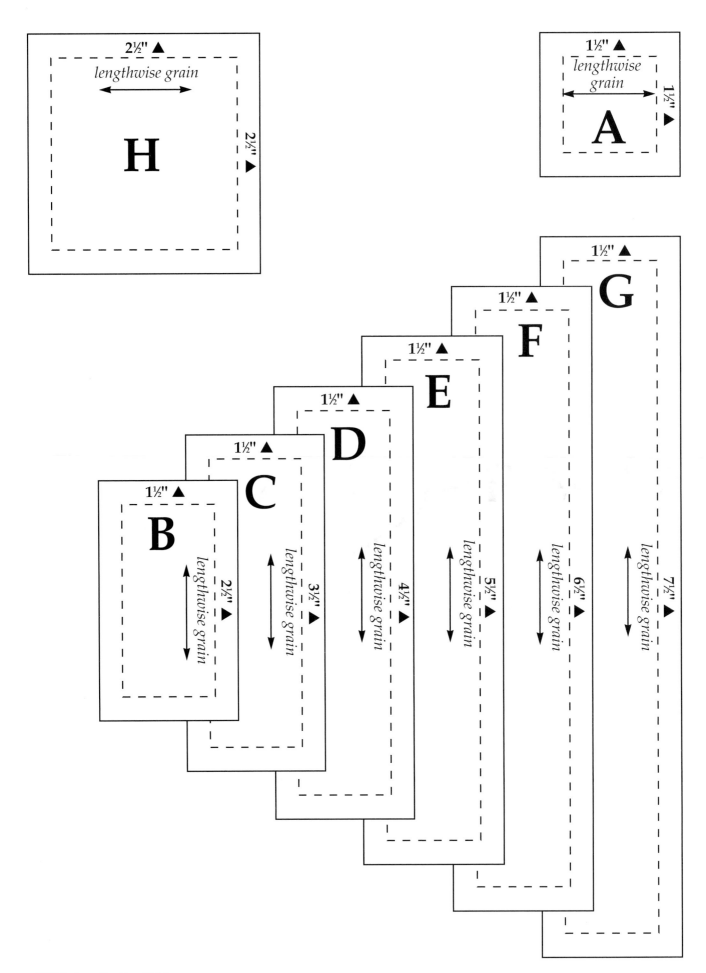

H
2½" ▲
lengthwise grain
2½" ▲

A
1½" ▲
lengthwise grain
1½" ▲

B
1½" ▲
lengthwise grain
2½" ▲

C
1½" ▲
lengthwise grain
3½" ▲

D
1½" ▲
lengthwise grain
4½" ▲

E
1½" ▲
lengthwise grain
5½" ▲

F
1½" ▲
lengthwise grain
6½" ▲

G
1½" ▲
lengthwise grain
7½" ▲

CHILD'S PLAY

Child's Play is the ideal pattern for turning no-sew quilt panels into real patchwork quilts. The 66" square quilt shown in the photograph on page 46 uses a single alphabet and teddy bear panel, border and all. The drawing below is for the 66" x 86" twin version. An 86" x 86" double or queen size coverlet is also presented. Look for a printed motif that can be framed in a 6" square. I've seen many fabrics that would be perfect in this quilt. Select colors from the print to set it off just so.

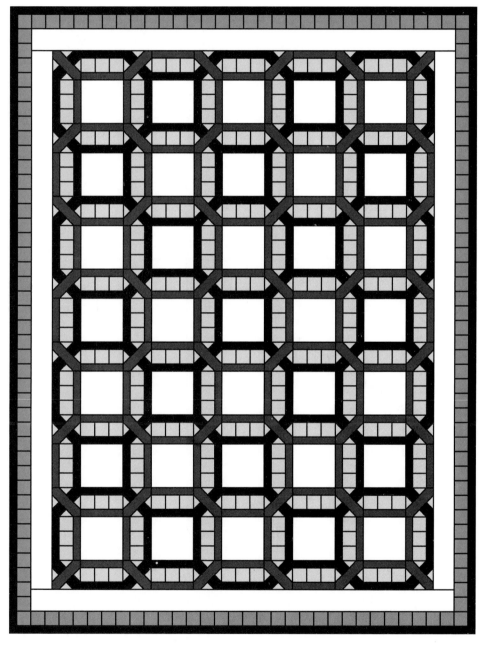

WHAT MAKES THIS QUILT EASY?

✔ The quilt achieves a Wedding Ring look of interlocking bands without curves and the fuss and bother they require.

✔ The no-sew picture blocks are simple, printed motifs--not appliqués or embroidery. Still, they are dressed up by the pieced setting, with its real patchwork, to make an extra-easy, extra-special quilt.

✔ Simple pieced border has no joints to match.

I made Child's Play in a quilt panel print that established the color scheme. I used bright and light primary colored prints with dark and medium blue sashes.

OTHER STUNNING COLORS

◆ Black and brown for the sashes; cream and light gold for the light squares and triangles; rust, eggplant, forest green, pumpkin, and turkey red for the border squares.

CHILD'S PLAY YARDAGE AND CUTTING REQUIREMENTS

Fabrics	Small - 66" x 66" No. Pcs.	Tot. Yds.	Patches	Medium - 66" x 86" No. Pcs.	Tot. Yds.	Patches	Large - 86" x 86" No. Pcs.	Tot. Yds.	Patches
Light Prints	18	1	144 D, 108 F	24	1¾	192 D, 246 F	38	2½	256 D, 336 F
Bright Prints	14	¾	124 F	24	¾	144 F	28	1	164 F
White Print (border)	1	*1⅞	25 A 2 @ 3½" x 60½" 2 @ 3½" x 54½"	1	2¼	35 A 2 @ 3½" x 74½" 2 @ 3½" x 60½"	1	3	49 A 2 @ 3½" x 80½" 2 @ 3½" x 74½"
Brt. Blue Print	1	1⅛	36 C, 60 E	1	1¾	48 C, 82 E	1	1¾	64 C, 112 E
Dk. Blue Print (border)	1	2	72 B, 60 E 2 @ 1½" x 66½" 2 @ 1½" x 64½"	1	2⅝	96 B, 82 E 2 @ 1½" x 84½" 2 @ 1½" x 66½"	1	2⅝	128 B, 112 E 2 @ 1½" x 86½" 2 @ 1½" x 84½"
(binding)		(2)	4 @ 1½" x 68"		(2⅝)	2 @ 1½" x 88" 2 @ 1½" x 68"		(2⅝)	4 @ 1½" x 88"
Lining Batting	1	4⅛	2 @ 35½" x 70" 70" x 70"	1	5¼	2 @ 35½" x 90" 70" x 90"	1	7⅞	3 @ 30½" x 90" 90" x 90"

AT-A-GLANCE ROTARY CUTTING OF STRIPS AND PATCHES

Fabrics	Strip Length	Strip Width	Cross Cuts	Add'l Cuts	Yield Per Strip	Number of Strips Needed Small	Med.	Large
Light Prints	9"	3¼"	2 @ 3¼"	⊠	8 D	18	24	32
	9"	2½"	3 @ 2½"	--	3 F	36	82	112
Bright Prints	9"	2½"	3 @ 2½"	--	3 F	42	48	55
White Print	20"	6½"	3 @ 6½"	--	3 A	9	12	17
Brt. Blue Print	18"	*C	45°, 3 @ 4½"	*C	3 C	12	16	22
	20"	1½"	3 @ 6½"	--	3 E	20	28	38
Dk. Blue Print	18"	*B	6 @ 2¾"	*B	6 B	10	14	19
	20"	1½"	3 @ 6½"	--	3 E	20	28	38

AT-A-GLANCE

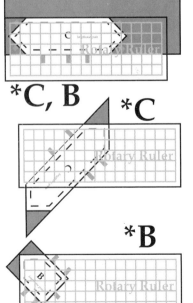

SPECIAL ROTARY CUTTING INSTRUCTIONS

✳ Note that you may need more of the white fabric than the listed amount if you plan to center a printed motif in the A patches. Buy enough to cut the required number of A squares. You may not be able to use each motif if they are printed closer together than 6½". Measure and count motifs to be sure.

⊠ For D triangles, indicated with this icon, cut strips and cross cuts as listed to make squares. Then make additional cuts across both diagonals, leaving the stacks of triangles right next to each other after the first diagonal cut.

✳C For C, tape the C pattern to your rotary ruler as shown, and cut strips from bright blue 18" long by the width of the C patch. (While C is taped to your ruler, cut strips from dark blue, as well. Set these aside for B's.) For C, cut off the lower right corner of a stack of strips at 45°. Position the 4½" line of your ruler at this angled cut, and cut along the ruler to make parallelograms. Continue cutting at 4½" intervals to make three stacks of parallelograms from each strip. Tape the C pattern to your rotary ruler as shown in the second figure. Align four sides of the pattern with a stack of parallelograms, and cut the point off. Rotate the fabric, realign the ruler, and cut again to complete a stack of C's.

✳B For B, use the dark blue strips cut with the C pattern, above. Cross cut at 2¾" intervals to make six rectangles per strip. Tape the B pattern to your ruler as shown. Align three sides of the pattern with the fabric rectangles, and cut off both corners to complete a stack of B's.

QUILT CONSTRUCTION

1 Sew a two different colored light print D triangles to a dark blue B to complete Unit 1 as shown. Press seam allowances toward the B patch. Repeat for all of the D's and B's to make the quantity indicated for your quilt size.

2 Sew two Unit 1's to a bright blue C patch to complete Unit 2 as shown. Press seam allowances toward the bright blue C patch. Repeat for all of the C's and Unit 1's to make the number listed for your quilt size. Set aside these units for Step 5.

3 Sew three F squares cut from three different light print fabrics in a row as shown to complete Unit 3. Press seam allowances to the right. Make the quantity indicated for your quilt size. You should have no leftover light print F's.

4 Sew a bright blue E rectangle to a Unit 3 as shown; sew a dark blue E to the opposite edge. Press seam allowances toward the rectangles. This completes Unit 4, the sash. Repeat for all Unit 3's and E's to make the number needed.

5 See the color photo on page 46 or the drawing on page 109. Arrange A patches, Unit 2's, and Unit 4's to make alternating sash rows and block rows as follows:

For the small quilt, the sash row has six Unit 2's alternated with five Unit 4's. The block row has six Unit 4's alternated with five A squares. The small quilt has six sash rows alternated with five block rows.

For the medium quilt, the sash row has six Unit 2's alternated with five Unit 4's. The block row has six Unit 4's alternated with five A squares. The medium quilt has eight sash rows alternated with seven block rows.

For the large quilt, the sash row has eight Unit 2's alternated with seven Unit 4's. The block row has eight Unit 4's alternated with seven A squares. The large quilt has eight sash rows alternated with seven block rows.

For all quilts, after you have laid out the entire quilt, turn the Unit 4's so that the A patch in the upper left corner is touching four bright blue E rectangles. Continue turning units so that each A patch is surrounded by four matching E rectangles. Squares surrounded by bright blue will alternate with squares surrounded by dark blue. Now turn the Unit 2's so that bright blue C patches touch bright blue E rectangles and dark blue B's touch dark blue E's. Adjust unit placement to achieve a good color balance. Put a label marked with the row number on the upper left corner of the leftmost unit in each row. Pick up the units and A patches for a row, stacking them in the order you have laid them out and keeping each turned properly. The leftmost unit should be on top. Make a separate stack for each row. Join the first two units of the first row in a seam. Similarly join the first unit and A patch of the second row. Now snip the thread chaining the first row to the second row. Add the next unit to the first row. Snip the thread chain and add the next unit to the second row. Proceed in this manner, always keeping the labeled unit on the left end, until the first two rows are complete. Proceed with the following pairs of rows until all rows are complete. Press seams toward the Unit 4's. Join rows in order. Oppose seams and pin at the corners of the units and A's. Press seam allowances toward the sash rows.

6 Add white side borders and trim them even with the quilt top. Add top and bottom borders and trim them even with the side borders. For the pieced borders, join bright F squares end to end. **For the small quilt,** you will need 30 F's for each side border and 32 F's for each of the top and bottom borders. **For the medium quilt,** you will need 40 F's for each side border and 32 F's for each of the top and bottom borders. **For the large quilt,** you will need 40 F's for each of the side borders and 42 F's for each of the top and bottom borders. Attach pieced side borders, then top and bottom borders. Next, add dark blue side borders and trim even with quilt top. Finally, add dark blue top and bottom borders and trim even with the side borders.

7 Seam the lining panels. Press the quilt top and lining well. Mark the quilting design of your choice in the A squares and white borders. Lay the lining face down and position the batting over it. Then center the quilt top, face up, over the batting and lining. Baste the layers together. Quilt in the ditch between all patches. Quilt the A squares and borders as marked. Bind to finish.

Unit 1
Make 72 (S),
Make 96 (M),
Make 128 (L).

Unit 2
Make 36 (S),
Make 48 (M),
Make 64 (L).

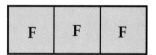

Unit 3
Make 60 (S),
Make 82 (M),
Make 112 (L).

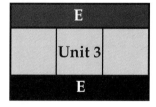

Unit 4
Make 60 (S),
Make 82 (M),
Make 112(L).

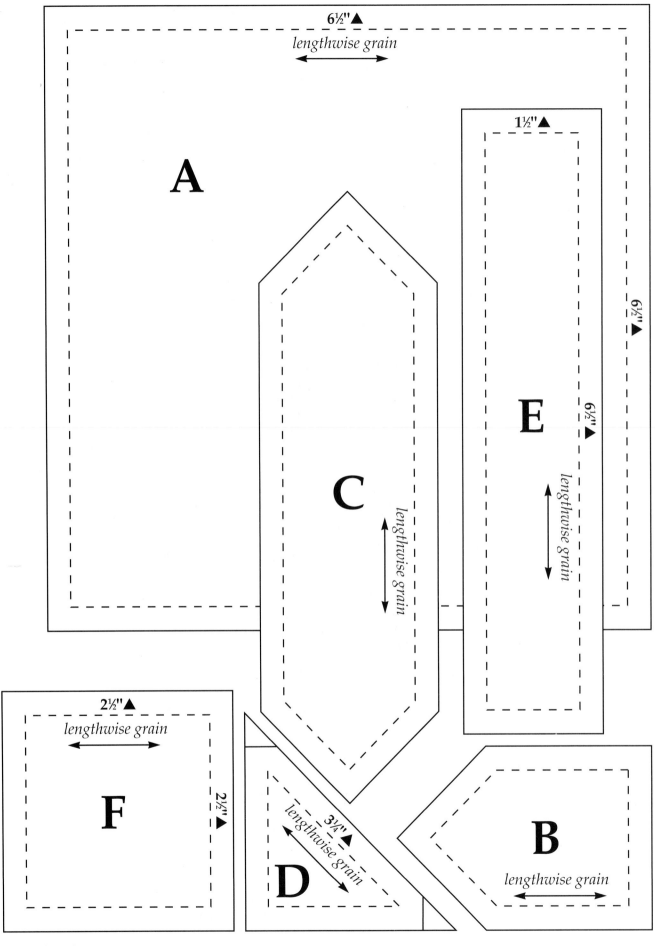

A

6½"▲
lengthwise grain

1½"▲

6½"▲

E

6½"▲

lengthwise grain

C

lengthwise grain

F

2½"▲
lengthwise grain

2½"▲

D

3¼"▲
lengthwise grain

B

lengthwise grain